Living Traditions

AT TEXAS A&M UNIVERSITY

Amy L. Bacon   Foreword by John J. Koldus III

TEXAS A&M UNIVERSITY PRESS, COLLEGE STATION

This paper meets the requirements of ANSI/NISO z39.48-1992
(Permanence of Paper).
Binding materials have been chosen for durability.

Library of Congress Cataloging-in-Publication Data

Bacon, Amy L., 1969–
    Building leaders, living traditions : the Memorial Student Center at
Texas A&M University / Amy L. Bacon ; foreword by John J. Koldus III. —1st ed.
        p. cm. — (Centennial series of the Association of Former
Students, Texas A&M University ; no. 110)
    Includes bibliographical references and index.
    ISBN-13: 978-1-60344-095-0 (cloth : alk. paper)
    ISBN-10: 1-60344-095-X (cloth : alk. paper)
    1. Texas A&M University. Memorial Student Center—History.
2. Student unions—Texas—College Station—History.   3. Student
activities—Texas—College Station—History.   I. Title.   II. Title:
Memorial Student Center at Texas A&M University.   III. Series.
LD5309.B33   2009
378.1'97—dc22
2008031064

To the sons and daughters of Texas A&M University
who have paid the ultimate sacrifice
in defense of our great nation:
The Memorial Student Center stands
forever in your honor and memory.

Contents

Illustrations

Foreword

A KEY TO THE STUDENT PERSONNEL APPROACH in higher education in recent history has been that every experience in which a student is involved can and should be an educational one. No group in higher education has promoted and supported this concept more on college campuses than the "student union."

Students are involved in every aspect of the operation, from budgeting and planning to serving as ushers for events. There are myriad student committees, one each for the major programs that occur each year. Staff members serve as advisors to each committee and in essence are the faculty involved in the educational process.

The student union on most campuses is an administrative subdivision of student personnel administration, that is, student services or student affairs. The facility housing that administrative unit, the student union, was often referred to as the "living room of the campus." The staff was responsible for providing a host of services, including guest rooms, dining facilities, recreational activities, study space, meeting room space, auditoriums, and especially for providing university-wide entertainment and educational programs. At Texas A&M University, the facility housing the student union was named the Memorial Student Center.

To accommodate the responsibilities relating to service, programming, and education, student union directors created a council to help plan, provide, and administer their programs. The council consisted of students, staff, faculty, and former students. As a faculty member at East Texas State University in the 1960s, I was invited to serve as a member of such a council. That experience served me well when I became the vice president for student services at East Texas State University and later at Texas A&M University, when I assumed the overall responsibility for the student union program.

My early introduction to the student union concept was presented by two excellent directors at East Texas State University, John Bernacki and Ron Robinson. Two of my early consultants in the profession were Dr. Bill Yardley, vice president for student affairs, and Bill Scott, director of the student union at the University of Houston. These two men were both instrumental in providing me with a clearer understanding of the role of the student union on campus. An interesting aside is that John Bernacki, Ron Robinson, and Bill Scott were all professional and personal friends of J. Wayne Stark, the student union director at Texas A&M University.

My relationship with the MSC was not limited to my association with the professional staff. Soon after I arrived on campus in 1973, with the aid of the Association of Former Students, I initiated a number of lunches and dinners with students. One of these was a 4:30 P.M. meal held every other week with the major student leaders on campus. The president of the Memorial Student Center Council, a student, held one of those leadership positions. I had the good fortune to become friends with each of the students who served as president of the MSC from 1973 to 1993. These students, along with the director, helped to keep me abreast of the programs, problems, and issues at the Memorial Student Center.

My role administratively at Texas A&M when I first arrived was to ensure that we had the best possible administrative professional in each of the directors' positions and to provide the best possible support to them in their endeavors. It didn't take me long to confirm that Wayne Stark was the best person for the position of director of the Memorial Student Center. We shared similar philosophical backgrounds and had a common interest and passion in the welfare and success of each individual student who attended Texas A&M University.

Years later, when Hal Gaines, the longtime associate director, planned to retire, I knew that Wayne was trying to replace Hal with a person who would succeed him as director. I told Wayne that he could not determine who would succeed him—that I would make that decision when the time arrived. I'm certain that comment fell on deaf ears. Wayne, after a lengthy, thorough search, selected Jim Reynolds as his associate director.

Jim, in essence, did have the inside track on following Wayne as the director because he was given the time and the responsibility to show that he was capable of handling the job. Over the years, Jim handled every assignment well and proved that he certainly deserved the director's position after Wayne retired. I know that Wayne was most pleased with my decision to promote Jim.

There is no way that I nor we—the Aggie family—can adequately thank Wayne Stark and Jim Reynolds for what they did to aid in the education of all Aggies who have or will ever attend Texas A&M University. Neither man ever sought any such recognition. Their lives, both personal and professional, were totally wrapped around the students involved in the MSC. They were both instrumental in encouraging students to be an integral part of the administrative jurisdiction of the program. They also encouraged students to travel, to seek educational experiences far beyond their personal sphere, and to seek careers previously considered unattainable. In essence, because of the magnitude of MSC programs, there is a little positive strand in each Aggie created by the contributions of two wonderful Memorial Student Center directors, Wayne Stark and Jim Reynolds, and their dedicated professional and student staffs.

My association with Amy Bacon dates back to her days in the late 1980s as an undergraduate student at Texas A&M University. My notes of that time remind me that she was bright, energetic, very personable, and dedicated to whatever endeavors she was involved in. This task, a daunting one, is a confirmation of those traits.

Let me thank Amy for: (1) initiating the project; (2) taking the time and effort to compile, document, and write the text; (3) exhibiting her appreciation of the excellent role that two respected and inspiring directors, Wayne Stark and Jim Reynolds, played in the ongoing success of the Memorial Student Center; and (4) outlining and espousing the role that the Memorial Student Center and its staff, both professional and student, played in the lives of so many Aggies.

I can personally attest to the difficulty that such a project entails. After I retired, I attempted to perform a similar historical chronology of the Division of Student Services at Texas A&M University from 1973 to 1993. I worked on that project for more than five years before finally succumbing to detail and documentation.

Congratulations, Amy on your perseverance, for creating a notable historical chronology of the Memorial Student Center, and for providing a reminder to all former students that we were most fortunate to share in the Aggie experience. Gig 'em, Aggies!

JOHN J. KOLDUS III

Preface

SINCE 2003, I have had the opportunity to research one of Texas A&M University's most cherished symbols—the Memorial Student Center. For me, it has truly been a labor of love, because the Memorial Student Center, or MSC, has had such a significant impact on shaping my A&M experience. Even as a little girl, I was always drawn to the MSC when my parents and I would visit my older brother, Craig Martin '84. It was usually one of the first stops we made, going into the awe-inspiring Flag Room, the bookstore where I would pick out my latest Aggie T-shirt, and down to the gameroom in the basement. On every visit, I was struck by how "active" the building was—filled with students, parents, and other visitors. Students sat behind tables lined up and down the crowded main hallway, promoting upcoming programs and activities, while huge banners hung from the ceiling doing the very same. I was always very fascinated to watch people remove their hats when entering the building, and my brother was quick to point out not to step on the grass or a cadet might tackle me.

When I entered A&M in 1987 as a freshman history major, I had already learned about the MSC at freshman orientation and Fish Camp, gaining a much deeper appreciation and reverence for its memorial status. Of course, the MSC was the place I knew to meet up with friends for lunch or grab a little study break away from my dorm room. By the end of my first year, I had became aware of the programs side of the MSC and was going to events such as *Cats,* brought by MSC OPAS, and the R.E.M. concert that MSC Town Hall sponsored, and hearing from friends who had gotten involved in MSC Hospitality, MSC Political Forum, and other committees. My curiosity was piqued, and then I saw an advertisement to apply for council assistant positions, which were for sophomores who would work with the various areas represented through the MSC Council. I applied, interviewed, and was selected to be a council assistant in the MSC Development area, which oversees all the fundraising of the various MSC committees. From that moment on, a whole new world opened up to me as I learned about the various MSC committees, the vast number of programs they produced, the large number of student volunteers who worked in the Student Programs Office (SPO) planning these programs, and the importance of fundraising through former students and foundations to help make these plans come to fruition. I was amazed to see this organization structured to run like a corporation and that students had direct responsibility for everything ranging from marketing and handling budget issues to securing speakers and arranging all their transportation. I personally became hooked on fundraising and found that I had a knack for asking people for money. I spent all my remaining years at A&M working my way up through the MSC organization to become the MSC vice president of development. Throughout my various positions, I gained self-confidence, became comfortable speaking in front of rooms full of people, and even learned how to fail and quickly pick myself up. I became active in other campus organizations, but most of my "other education" significantly revolved around the MSC. It opened doors for me to meet numerous successful former students, dignitaries, entertainers, university administrators, members of the Board of Regents, and A&M presidents, and it even helped me land my first job out of college in the fundraising field.

Jane Bailey, assistant to the MSC director, recalls me saying as a student that one day I would write a book about this special place. Being a history major, I thought it would be interesting to write about the building and its programs. Of course, after a fundraising career, graduate school, marriage, a couple of other fundraising jobs, and starting a family, it was not until the MSC celebrated its fiftieth anniversary in 2001 that the idea came back to me. In 2003, I began a four-year journey, researching what I believe is a unique part of the Aggie experience and one whose impact on students and the university has not fully been explored. There have been some attempts in various university publications to give a chronology of the MSC, particularly in regard to its multiple renovations, and to discuss the importance of the student center as a memorial to fallen Aggies and as the "living room" of the campus. Yet, in this narrative, I hope to provide an introspective look at the history of the MSC against the backdrop of the university's transformation from a rural, all-male military college to the world-class institution it is today. What becomes very clear is that the MSC has very distinct roles and meanings to different people. The student center tells us important things about the university and the A&M culture. After interviewing more than eighty former students, A&M administrators, and past MSC and A&M staff members, I had no doubt that the building and the people who have worked within its walls ultimately shaped the Texas A&M we see today. The way in which the MSC has affected the university and shaped its culture is the story that follows.

I owe a great deal to so many people who have helped me from the very beginning with this project. James R. "Jim" Reynolds, Jane Bailey, and Luke Altendorf gave me such tremendous assistance and encouragement to take on this endeavor, providing me resources, names, photographs, and trails to follow in finding documents and information. Their amazing knowledge and recollection of institutional history have been invaluable, and I would not have been able to do this without them. Members of the MSC staff have been particularly helpful, especially Monica Davis, Anne Black, Terri Becker, Sarah Nash, Deryle Richmond, Dave Salmon, and Karen Dolliver. Dr. Dean Bresciani and his staff in the office of the vice president for student affairs provided auspicious support, and I am especially thankful to him and Brian Hervey '92 for their wonderful enthusiasm for the project.

In searching for documents and sources, I am extremely grateful to David L. Chapman '67 and his staff at the Cushing Memorial Library and Archives at Texas A&M University for maintaining the extensive documentary history of Texas A&M and making it readily available to me. I especially want to thank Valerie Coleman and the entire Cushing staff for tolerating my visits and for all their help in pulling out boxes upon boxes of historical documents, photographs, and other resources. I would also like to extend my gratitude to Porter Garner '77 and the staff of the Association of Former Students for finding old *Texas Aggie* magazine articles and agendas and minutes from Board of Directors meetings, particularly those dealing with the creation of the A&M Development Fund in 1942 and its role in building the MSC.

The more than eighty interviews I conducted with former students, administrators, staff, and friends of the MSC and Texas A&M were my favorite part of the research for this book because I got the opportunity to meet such phenomenal Aggies, hear their stories and firsthand accounts, and gain tremendous insight into the influence the MSC has had on the evolution of Texas A&M. John H. Lindsey '44, R. N. "Dick" Conolly '39, and Dick Hervey '42 provided wonderful glimpses of the A&M campus prior to the MSC's establishment and really set the stage for me to better understand the early days of J. Wayne Stark, the first MSC director. Dr. John J. Koldus III was extremely helpful with his unique perspective and knowledge of the MSC's role during his twenty-year tenure as vice president for student services. Everyone I interviewed was so supportive and had such a positive response to the project, it continued to reaffirm in my mind that this was a history needing to be told. I want to thank all of them for their participation. I also want to extend my sincere appreciation to Dr. Paul J. Springer '97, who transcribed all the interview tapes and did a magnificent job. The book would have been impossible to write without his painstaking efforts.

I also owe special thanks to Dr. Joseph A. Pratt, my former graduate professor and advisor at the University of Houston, who allowed me the opportunity to brainstorm with him on my early thoughts for the project and provided a great deal of guidance and advice. Many, many friends and others have extended their support in numerous ways. They include Marlene Bacon, Stephanie Stock, Mary Ann and Bill Shallberg, Jerry Clark, Nancy Hough, George and Liz McMillin, Marc Carroll '91, Dallas Shipp '03, Allen and Janet Flynt '86, Susan Kent '90, Jason Wilcox '91, Ed Valicek '91, and Laura Sickmen '90, who was forced to endure reading through one of the early drafts of the manuscript. To these and many others who go unnamed, I am very grateful.

I would never have attempted to do such a large-scale project had it not been for the love, support, presence, and encouragement of God and my family. My grandmother, Amy Lois Dever, was an avid reader and, along with my mother, she instilled a love of reading and history in me. Although she passed away a couple of years into the project, I know she would be very proud to have her namesake be an author. My parents, Bobby and Sue Martin, gave me wonderful encouragement and helped in so many ways throughout this process, including taking care of my most valuable treasure—my daughter Ellie—when I had to do interviews or make research trips to College Station. I owe Ellie so much for enduring countless hours of me working on the computer, as well as many days and nights without me. She was such a trouper through it all and a wonderful cheerleader, sharing her mother so I could fulfill this dream. And, none of this would have happened without the love and support of Robert, my husband, who endlessly proofread and offered ideas and suggestions but most importantly, helped me believe that I should be the one to tell the MSC's story.

AMY L. BACON '91

BUILDING LEADERS, LIVING TRADITIONS

Introduction

NO TRIP TO TEXAS A&M UNIVERSITY would be complete without a visit to the Memorial Student Center—"the living room" of the A&M campus. The student center, or the MSC, as it is commonly known, draws in thousands of students, visitors, and former students through its welcoming doors whether they are attending a football game at Kyle Field, looking for that perfect Aggie T-shirt, or taking a walking tour of the campus. At the MSC, Aggies gather to meet friends in its grand Flag Room or at the bookstore. On a couch in one of its hidden nooks, weary students might be seen catching a quick rest before their next class. In the Student Programs Office on the second floor, more than eighteen hundred Aggie students devote their time and energy to producing fourteen hundred student-led programs annually for the A&M campus and surrounding community. Of course, before ever entering the building, they must first remove their hats and refrain from walking on the surrounding grass, for the MSC is a memorial dedicated to those Aggies who gave their lives to defend this great nation. Yet no matter what brings a person into the MSC, one quickly becomes aware that this is indeed a very special place because it is not only the social epicenter of the A&M campus but also a significant part of the Aggie experience.

First and foremost, all Aggies uphold the MSC as a memorial to those fellow students who sacrificed their lives for freedom. The student center was dedicated in 1951 as a "living, useful memorial" to honor those Aggies who died in World Wars I and II. For some Aggies, the MSC is simply the A&M community center, the main gathering place to meet friends, have a meal, pick up one's mail, or find a special Aggie souvenir in the bookstore. It is the central building on campus and provides amenities and service facilities to students, former students, and visitors. For others, the MSC holds a different meaning, serving as a primary provider of the "other education" at A&M—valuable experience students gain through cultural, recreational, leadership, and service opportunities afforded outside the classroom. The MSC has an established tradition of sponsoring campuswide programs for A&M students and the surrounding community. Whether it be a political program, an art exhibit, or a film series, the MSC has been the home for such programs. Yet the MSC means something even more to Aggie students who do the actual planning of such programs. To them, the MSC is a leadership laboratory in which they learn how to prepare, raise funds for, and implement leadership conferences, speaker series, and visual and performing arts programs, as well as to operate the MSC as an organization. Whether viewing the MSC through one of these lenses or a combination of several, there is no doubt the Memorial Student Center has had a significant impact on the university's history and culture through these four roles— beloved memorial, community center for the university and surrounding Bryan–College Station area, student programming agent, and leadership laboratory. In many ways, the MSC—as a building and through its staff, student leadership, and programs—has served as a catalyst for changes that would ultimately have to take place at A&M to transform it from the rural, all-male military college of its past to the vast, world-class institution it is today, serving more than forty-five thousand diverse students.

When the Agricultural and Mechanical College of Texas opened in 1876 after being created as a land-grant institution by the Morrill Act of 1862, no one could possibly have envisioned the campus that exists today on what was then a remote, wind-swept prairie. The Corps of Cadets, first established through a mandate of the Morrill Act to include "military tactics" with instruction, was the sole way of life at A&M— the educational, military, recreational, and social focus of the college. The campus reflected this through its very utilitarian, bleak buildings constructed to provide classrooms, dormitory rooms, a mess hall, and apartments for administrators and faculty. Although modern conveniences became more prevalent in society over time, these new amenities were not readily found on the A&M campus. Even though additional buildings were constructed, a few of which were intended to serve as a social center for the college, such as the YMCA Building and the Aggieland

Inn, it was not until 1950 that A&M finally received its much anticipated Memorial Student Center. Students and former students had worked tirelessly during the previous twenty years to push for the building of a student union, and they had mounted fundraising campaigns to make the dream a reality. When its doors opened, no one on the A&M campus could have imagined a more impressive and thoroughly modern building. The MSC was one of the campus's first air-conditioned buildings, and it was considered contemporary in design and "elegantly appointed." Its state-of-the-art amenities included a main lounge, gift shop, dining room, coffee shop, telephone center, record room, browsing library, gameroom, ballroom, meeting and assembly rooms, bowling alley, and a sixty-six-room hotel. George Sessions Perry, author of *The Story of Texas A and M,* writes in 1951 that if the MSC "inclined to rock to and fro a bit, it would more closely approximate the first-class accommodations on a luxury liner." Over the next fifty-five years, and through several expansions and renovations to its facilities, the MSC has faithfully served as A&M's community center, the most well-known gathering place on campus for all Aggies.[1]

Further enhancing its role as A&M's social center, the MSC has a rich tradition of being a critical source of campuswide programming. The first MSC director, J. Wayne Stark '39, envisioned this role for the MSC as far back as 1947. He believed the MSC should be the primary entity that exposed Aggies to a host of programs that broadened their worldview—art, poetry, music, theatre, dancing, politics, and travel—all concepts and programs not likely stressed within a rural, conservative, all-male military college in the 1940s. But from the very beginning, "Mr. Stark" fervently strived to bring a diverse array of visual arts, worldviews, and cultural exchanges so students might gain exposure to the world outside the Corps of Cadets, beyond Texas A&M and their hometowns. Early programs such as MSC Great Issues, MSC Travel, and MSC SCONA (Student Conference on National Affairs), and others not only gave Aggies the opportunity to learn and question the world around them but also played a significant role, as would later programs, in generating national recognition for Texas A&M. When Stark, Jim Reynolds (the second MSC director), and Aggie students began approaching successful, well-known individuals in their specific fields and inviting them to participate in various MSC programs, more and more people gained exposure to the unique setting and spirit of the university. Many programs, such as MSC SCONA, MSC Great Issues, the MSC Wiley Lecture Series, MSC OPAS (Opera and Performing Arts Society), and MSC Town Hall concerts, put A&M on the map and brought national recognition to the university. Programs incorporating renowned heads of state and performers, including former presidents George H. W. Bush and Jimmy Carter, British prime minister Margaret Thatcher, Soviet president Mikhail Gorbachev, dancer Rudolf Nureyev, and the Bolshoi Ballet, combined to create an open, welcoming environment at A&M for dignitaries. The MSC, in its role as a provider of quality campus programs, ultimately helped the university make great strides in projecting the image of a world-class university.[2]

The secret to the success of MSC programs lies with the students who produce them, and again, this is the way in which numerous Aggies look upon the MSC, as a place for student development and leadership training. Today, the MSC is considered to be one of the largest student-led programming entities in the United States. Early on, Stark wanted to create an environment where students could be given the unique chance, unlike anything they experienced in the classroom, to plan programs and develop as leaders. He knew the Corps of Cadets spirit and the military culture of A&M had created a fertile ground on which to provide an enhanced form of leadership development. Stark set up student-staff governance of the MSC and its programs, giving students the opportunity to completely plan and implement quality cultural, educational, social, recreational, and leadership programs, as well as manage business-related issues and the challenges of running the MSC organization. Such practical experience, as well as the accompanying exposure to art, culture, social graces, political forums, international travel, and leadership development the MSC provided, would level the playing field for Aggies out in the real world. Stark's grandson, Drew McGehee '93, believes he wanted to give students the opportunity "to be involved in things they could not possibly have ever imagined they would be involved with before they came to A&M."[3]

An important outcome of both the leadership development occurring in the MSC and Stark's zealous determination to see Aggies dream big dreams resulted in doors opening for Aggies in graduate education. These were doors typically closed or goals not considered attainable. Stark utilized MSC programs, many of which brought successful former students, heads of state, politicians, and leaders in business and law to the A&M campus, as a vehicle to create an extensive network. When he identified students as having leadership potential, he encouraged them to pursue lofty goals such as attaining advanced degrees at prestigious universities, including Harvard Business School, or applying for international internships. As Frank M. Muller Jr. '65, a former student body president, explains, Stark had the ability to "push students in ways that they never dreamed possible . . . pushing them to spend a year overseas, pushing them hard to spend their summers in places they could not even

spell, and pushing them to do things and try for leadership positions they never would have even considered."[4] Over time, he created a vast group of former students, whom he could call upon to mentor and place "Stark's boys" in graduate programs or jobs that would advance their goals. Stark formed a networking base of Aggies all over the world in every type of business, and many consider him the most prolific creator of the "Aggie Network." Through Stark's expansive network (one Reynolds inherited and built upon), Aggies have received opportunities immeasurable in scope and significance—opportunities historically not associated with "Aggies." Former MSCers have become influential players in law and Fortune 500 businesses as well as state and national politics. A "who's who" of Texas A&M is very likely today to include "Starkies" and many former MSCers. This phenomenal group of former students continues to be one of the most remarkable by-products of the MSC.[5]

On Muster day in 1951, Tyree Bell '13, president of the A&M Board of Directors, remarked at the MSC's formal dedication that the "magnificent edifice you see here will always serve as a shrine of memories and as a setting for that jewel we call the 'A&M Spirit.'"[6] Exposure to the "other education," leadership development, the Aggie network, student pro-

Weekday traffic outside the south entrance of the Memorial Student Center and Joe Routt Boulevard, c. 2008. Courtesy Memorial Student Center Director's Office

gramming opportunities, remembering those Aggies who have fallen in service to their country—all of these are part of the unique Aggie experience, and all of these are found within the walls of the Memorial Student Center. The MSC, as a memorial, a community center, a purveyor of campus programming, and leadership laboratory, has a longstanding, proven history of stepping up to meet the needs of a changing A&M. The narrative that follows shows how the history of the MSC and the university are inextricably interwoven. It is a story that not only chronicles the evolution of the MSC's facilities, programs, and student leadership opportunities but also reveals how the MSC played an active role in the transformation of A&M and how it continues to be significant to the university's future.

ONE

A Dream Comes True

THE MSC'S EARLY BEGINNINGS, 1918–51

TO UNDERSTAND THE IMPORTANCE of how the Memorial Student Center originated, one must first take a closer look at cadet life and the A&M campus prior to the MSC's establishment. At its founding in 1876, the all-male Agricultural and Mechanical College of Texas was situated on a barren prairie with only two buildings—Old Main and Gathright Hall. At the time, Brazos County was considered one of the poorest, most isolated counties in Texas. The campus was accessible only by horseback and stagecoach or by train, but only as far as Hearne or Hempstead. The frontierlike environment, with wolves and other wild animals roaming the campus, made A&M a very unattractive destination. John A. Adams Jr. paints a desolate picture in his book, *Keepers of the Spirit: The Corps of Cadets at Texas A&M University, 1876–2001,* citing the lack of adequate amenities: "no running water, no electricity, no streets, and no sanitary toilets." One state senator at the time wrote that he "had rather give his boy a pony, a six-shooter, bottle of whiskey and deck of cards and start him out to get his education than send him to A&MC."[1]

With military training a requirement for all students, the Corps of Cadets was the only way of life on the campus, and it was a rough one indeed. Students had to study by kerosene oil lamps, pump and carry water from nearby wells, and cut their own timber for firewood. Cadets gained an education in agriculture, "mechanics" or engineering, military tactics, languages, and literature while living under strict military organization and discipline. Organized extracurricular activities were nonexistent, and the students had to carve out their own forms of non-military activity. They could not even leave campus without permission. Therefore, in many ways, the Corps was at the center of everything that occurred on campus—educationally, militarily, and socially. It is interesting to note that even though the college and its students were both rugged in nature, the cadets formed some early student organizations that stressed the classical and literary arts. When Lawrence Sullivan Ross became president of the A&M college in 1891, he further promoted the development of additional student organizations, including the band, orchestra, a cadet glee club (later to become known as the Singing Cadets), and even a football team. In the early 1900s, campus dance clubs were formed to establish some semblance of social life on the campus, with the women of the college (the wives and daughters of the college presidents and faculty) hosting periodic social events. So while the A&M college still existed in what many considered a frontierlike environment, members of the Corps, as well as some college administrators, took it upon themselves to develop social and recreational activities on the campus to ease some of the drudgery existing in the very strict, military-style life of a cadet. Yet what became very apparent over time and as more organizations arose was the lack of one center where all these activities converged. The campus dynamic was about to change, though, as colleges nationwide and internationally were finding their own answer to this problem through the creation of college unions.[2]

The origins of the college union concept go back to the organized efforts of university debating societies in England. In 1812, a small circle of students at Oxford University in England, led by Augustus Hare, formed a group known as the Attic Society with the intent to create a forum for free discussion and debate. Similar debate societies developed at Oxford and spread to Cambridge University, where their needs for facilities, services, and organizational structure increased. As a result, the college union idea became formalized at Cambridge University in 1815 when these debate societies collectively formed a "union" to meet their desire for space and other amenities. Oxford established a similar organization in 1823, and the "Oxford Union" soon became the only place for students to debate political issues on campus. Members of the Oxford Union, as well as those at Cambridge, debated not only each other but also the political statesmen and great thinkers of the country. Members who went on to become distinguished political leaders in both England and internationally received their parliamentary training in these organizations. However, over time, these unions became more than just debating societies. The Oxford Union consisted of buildings and grounds that included a debate hall, a reading and reference library, dining rooms, and a billiard room, while the Cambridge Union had similar facilities, including a club room or bar. John Corbin, an American at Oxford in 1902, described its union as "the epitome of all the best elements of Oxford life. The library was filled with men reading or working at special hobbies; the reading and smoking rooms were crowded; the lawn was daily thronged with undergraduates gossiping over a cup of tea . . . in a word, the Union held the elect of Oxford, intellectual, social, and sporting."[3]

By 1895, the college union idea had spread across the Atlantic to higher education in the United States, beginning with the Harvard Union and the construction of the first student union building at the University of Pennsylvania.[4] This facility, Houston Hall, contained many amenities for the students, including a swimming pool and baths, gymnasium, bowling alleys, pool and chess tables, lunch counters, reading and writing rooms, an auditorium, and separate rooms for the use of committees such as the Athletic Association and the Young Men's Christian Association (YMCA). The popular YMCA movement had spread across the nation and made it possible for students to swim and play basketball and volleyball in Y buildings on college campuses, but such facilities were slowly being displaced by the building of student unions. Over the next twenty years, student unions cropped up at Brown University, Ohio State University, the flagship universities of Michigan, Wisconsin, Illinois, and Indiana, and at other institutions. The American college union adopted primarily the characteristics of a social center—a place to meet friends and a place to dine. Porter Butts, a leader in the college union field and director of the Wisconsin Union from 1927 to 1968, wrote that student unions in the United States had "become social-cultural centers embracing the interests of the total university community of students and faculty."[5]

By the 1920s, several factors contributed to student unions evolving into these campus community centers. First, the success of the women's suffrage movement had chipped away at the longstanding tradition of education for men only as well as the notion of separate educational facilities. Men and women had begun to find it odd that they must view each other from separate educational worlds. As a result, student unions began opening their doors to everyone. No longer were these facilities solely male domains. Men and women could come together under one roof to dine, participate in social activities, and for recreation. Also, World War I directly affected the development of student unions across

American campuses. Enrollment surged dramatically after the war, and students were forced into small, cramped rooming houses devoid of social niceties or dining facilities. The war canteens and recreation centers used by servicemen away from home served as models for colleges to emulate through their campus counterpart—the student union. In numerous cases, raising money for such a building also became tied to the war itself. As Butts pointed out in an address concerning the history and goals of the college union, "What better type of living memorial to honor those who served in the war?" Yet on the A&M campus, these national trends in student unions would take nearly thirty years to come to fruition and in the case of coeducation, much longer.[6]

Events of the war did, however, set the initial idea in motion. Texas A&M contributed significantly to World War I by supplying 1,233 officers and 984 noncommissioned former students and cadets. By the end of the war in 1918, 53 Aggies had lost their lives in the conflict. President William B. Bizzell sought a way to memorialize these Aggies, and in November 1918, he envisioned a "more dignified, elaborate and permanent memorial that shall be made to perform some useful function on the campus at the same time that it perpetuates the names of the men who gave up their lives for freedom." He invited suggestions from alumni, and they offered ideas such as a memorial library, a new "Memorial Football Stadium," and a student activities building. Alumni probably had little knowledge of all that the student union concept entailed, but apparently this was the first time a request for a student activities building was put forward in writing. It seems the need for such a central location where students could meet informally to relax and entertain visitors had become more evident for the growing college, although there were other places on campus trying to fulfill this role—the YMCA Building and later the Aggieland Inn.[7]

Since 1914, the YMCA Building had served as the center of campus social life, being somewhat of an informal gathering place for students. In conjunction with the popular YMCA movement spreading across the nation, Colonel Edward B. Cushing '80 organized the effort to build a YMCA on the A&M campus, raising funds for construction, including a pledge of thirty thousand dollars from John D. Rockefeller. When the YMCA opened its doors in 1914, it provided students with reading rooms, Bible study rooms, a tiled swimming pool, dining room, kitchen, alumni association rooms, auditorium, and bowling alleys. It also provided an amenity previously unheard of on campus—a women's restroom. Later on, a soda fountain was added where Aggies bought candy, ice cream, and fountain drinks. Along with another building, the Aggieland Inn, these two facilities did their best to provide some semblance

of a homelike atmosphere on the campus. The inn, once located across Houston Street from Sbisa Hall, was built in 1925 and served as the only place on campus to accommodate parents, sweethearts, and visitors. It contained thirty-six guest rooms, a large dining room, coffee shop, cafeteria, and a kitchen. The cadets considered it a treat to have a home-cooked Sunday dinner at the inn, and the coffee shop was open twenty-four hours a day.[8]

By late 1919, the vision of a student center and a library gave way to the momentum generated by the proposal to raise money for a new "concrete" football stadium. Construction never materialized and the project was indefinitely delayed. Yet the call for a student center could again be heard in the mid-1930s as the college continued to experience increased enrollment. In 1934–1935, enrollment totaled 2,998 cadets. For the term of 1935–1936, enrollment increased to 3,430 and there was a steady growth pattern—4,075 in September 1936 and more than 4,400 cadets by January 1937.[9] With this wealth of students, problems arose, such as overcrowding and the lack of on-campus student facilities. Editorials surfaced in the *Battalion* in 1936–1937 addressing the need for a "union building," particularly at the time of year when more dances

From 1914 till the opening of the MSC in 1950, the YMCA Building was the closest thing to a student union on campus. It housed "Casey's Confectionery," a popular campus hangout. Courtesy Cushing Memorial Library and Archives

The Aggieland Inn was the other social center on campus before 1950, playing host to parents, sweethearts, and other visitors to A&M. With the opening of the MSC, the inn's kitchen and dining room closed down and the building was finally razed in 1965.
Courtesy Cushing Memorial Library and Archives

and weekend visitors came to A&M. As one editor wrote, "We are again brought face to face with the acute need of a Union building for A and M college. And we believe it is time something be done about it."[10] Students complained of the cramped "barnlike" assembly hall as a poor setting for plays and shows. They argued that the expansive mess hall, while functional in this particular role, made a very poor dance hall when trying to decorate it for an event or listen to music. It did not help matters when the Texas Union on the University of Texas campus opened in 1933, with lounges, meeting rooms, student organization offices, and a ballroom. Of course, the problem in constructing such a facility was the lack of funds, but the students recognized this was a hurdle they would have to jump in order to get their union building. The *Battalion* editor placed this responsibility squarely on the student body, challenging them to raise money and have it matched by former students interested in supporting the concept. Students acknowledged that the amount of money they could raise would be only a small start, but they understood the significance of such a movement, especially by showing their willingness to spend their time, effort, and own money on a student center they would not see built during their time at A&M. In a letter to his fellow cadets, Jeff Horn '37, YMCA president, encouraged Aggies to "not sit back and beg—let's do something" as he challenged them to contribute ten dollars each to a student union building fund set up at the fiscal department. The classes of 1936 and 1937 met the challenge by collecting money and donating those funds as their class gifts.[11]

Urged on by their Aggie sons, the Bell County A&M Mothers' Club (now known as the East Bell County Mothers' Club) took a great interest in having a student union built. In 1937, Florence Brewster, the club's president, and her executive board drew up a resolution calling for the construction of a student union building. Their resolution called for the establishment of a special fund at a local bank where Aggies could contribute toward the building of a student center. In an effort to get more people on board with the concept, the resolution was sent out to all existing Aggie clubs, Aggie Mothers' Clubs, the college's administration, and the Board of Directors. The Bell County A&M Mothers' Club made the first donation, in the amount of six dollars, and contributions came in steadily thereafter.[12]

The next big push for a student union building came in the 1940s, a period marked by thousands of Aggies serving around the globe in World War II and followed by a tremendous enrollment increase on the A&M campus. From 1938 to 1942, the student body had grown to more than sixty-five hundred, but this number declined to fewer than nineteen hundred by 1944. By 1946, more than nine thousand new students and returning veterans descended upon Aggieland.[13] In an effort to increase support to the college and the growing number of former students, the Association of Former Students abolished membership dues in 1942 and instead established the A&M Development Fund (later to become the Annual Fund). By way of this fund, the association picked up the mantle students had given them to support the dream of a student union building. The association asked every former student to make an annual gift to this fund, with the first goal of this fund to provide contributions for the future construction of a "Student Activities Center." In his Muster address of 1943, association president William J. Lawson spoke of a center that would "provide more than the conventional social pleasures of the Union Buildings that most big schools enjoy, a Center that will provide facilities for wholesome recreation, physical development, accommodations for visiting ex-students, parents, and sweethearts, and a cultural background that our campus has lacked." The goal for 1943 was to raise fifty thousand dollars to be placed in war bonds for the duration, and that sum would then be available to "launch the Memorial Student Activity Center."[14] It appears that the decision to designate the facility as a memorial was a holdover from the initial concept in 1918 and by 1943 was even more timely given the sacrifices so many Aggies were making abroad in the various theaters of World War II.

By 1946, a group of students, faculty, staff, and former students began to study seriously the feasibility of a student union building. They enlisted the services of Porter Butts, the nationally recognized director of the college union at the University of Wisconsin, to provide observations and suggestions. Butts noted that A&M presented a "unique need and opportunity in Union planning" due to the fact the campus lacked many of the characteristic amenities found at other colleges. While conducting conferences with this group in July 1946, he observed the campus's rural isolation and the absence of a typical "college town" environment with services and recreation outlets, as well as the lack of women students. He noted that while the college halls on campus provided for the housing and feeding of students, they did not offer social facilities. Although the YMCA Building and the Aggieland Inn somewhat made up for these shortcomings at the college, there simply was no centralized, comfortable gathering place on campus, no "hearthstone" or "living room." He also believed the heavy emphasis on training for engineering and agriculture minimized the importance and opportunity for cultural subjects to be added to the curriculum and saw that a student union could fill that gap. Most importantly, he believed, the creation of a student union could "parallel training for military leadership with informal training for, and in practice in, citizenship leadership." Therefore, he saw the establishment of a student center as vitally important to A&M if it was done in such a way as to not be just a club building but rather a "plan for campus life" and a vehicle for the "full-rounded development of students."[15]

As a result of Butts's recommendations, President Gibb Gilchrist officially appointed the Union Committee to conduct a study of the facilities needed in the building, the operation and control of the building, its financing, and its programs. The committee, headed by E. E. McQuillen, executive director of the Association of Former Students, recommended the construction of a student union building to start no later than May 1, 1948, with a projected completion date of September 1949. The Texas A&M System architect, Carleton Adams, who also served on the Union Committee, had already made several trips to other college unions around the country and had developed an architectural design incorporating many of his observations and the suggestions of Porter Butts. The committee also acknowledged that the minimum facilities needed in such a building could not be provided for less than $1.5 million. As of 1947, there was $823,160 available in the Union Building Fund, with nearly $280,000 having been contributed by the Association of Former Students. More than eleven thousand Aggies had donated to the fund, thus indicating their agreement that this facility was indeed a priority.[16] President Gilchrist recommended to the Board of Directors that the rest of the funding be augmented by either a bond issue or through the allocation of funds from sources available to the board. As for the organization and operation of the student union building, the committee recommended there be a policy-forming union advisory committee, composed of representatives from the student body, staff, and former students. In addition, the committee saw the need for a program

J. Wayne Stark, the first director of the MSC, pictured at his desk in 1954–55. Courtesy Memorial Student Center Director's Office

and activities committee, largely comprised of students, which would plan and supervise the day-to-day programs and activities of the building, thus serving as the "working organization of the Union program." A union director would then work with this committee and under the Union Advisory Committee. McQuillen '20 and other members of this committee spent considerable time looking for the person best suited to the director's position. The names of several experienced individuals were brought forward, but in 1947, President Gilchrist named A&M former student J. Wayne Stark '39 as the first director of the soon-to-be built student center.[17]

Although born in Lamesa, Texas, Stark grew up in the small town of Winters, south of Abilene. While attending Texas A&M, he served as associate editor of the *Battalion* for two years, club editor of the *Longhorn* (as the yearbook was titled at the time), president of the Glee Club, and president of the Biology Club. He received a bachelor of arts degree in history in 1939. During the fall that year, he enrolled at the University of Texas law school but withdrew in 1941 when called to active duty in World War II. In 1942, Stark married Jean Stinson of Conroe, Texas, who worked for Humble Oil and Refining Company as an evaluation engineer. After his military service, Stark worked for two years at Anderson, Clayton, and Company, a corporation regarded at the time as the largest buyer, seller, storer, and shipper of raw cotton. Dick Hervey '42 recalls that he, Stark, and two other former students applied for the job as executive director of the Association of Former Students in 1947, following E. E. McQuillen's departure to assume the directorship of the Texas A&M Development Fund. Hervey was selected for the position, but another position at the university was just being created—director of the student center. According to Hervey, E. L. Angell, assistant to President Gilchrist, encouraged Stark to apply for the job, and Hervey believes Angell had a direct influence on Stark's being awarded the director position by Gilchrist.[18]

Stark began working as the director in 1947, before the first spade of earth had even been turned. In order to study a variety of facilities and their student programs, he traveled to numerous student unions, particularly in the Midwest, including the student centers at Purdue University, the University of Minnesota, and the University of Illinois. Perhaps more than any other student union, the Wisconsin Union impressed Stark the most. This union's wide array of services and student programming opportunities gave Stark insight into how a student center could serve as much more than just a place where students could "come in out of the rain, use the restrooms, and get a drink."[19] He caught a glimpse of what A&M could gain through a similar student center, and his broad vision began to take shape. His observations, along with those of Carleton Adams, were incorporated into the final design for the building. The plans for the three-story student center included a main lounge, dining room, coffee shop, telephone center, gameroom, browsing library, record room, various sitting areas, four darkrooms and an art room, sixty-six hotel guest rooms, a bowling alley, numerous meeting rooms,

University president Frank Bolton makes his remarks at the MSC groundbreaking held on September 21, 1948. Courtesy Cushing Memorial Library and Archives

a gift shop, and a soda fountain. In addition, there were several work-rooms for student committees of the center, as well as an office for the Association of Former Students executive director.[20]

First and foremost, the student center would be designated as a memorial to those Aggies who lost their lives in the two world wars. Many student unions across the country were either named or being renamed as "memorial" student unions right after World War I and then again following the end of World War II. While President Bizzell first brought forth the idea of having a student center as a memorial in 1918, it is likely that subsequent administrations always kept this memo-rial concept in the back of their minds should funds become available and they were able to move forward in building such a facility. Finally, on September 21, 1948, the dream became a reality as the long-awaited construction of the Memorial Student Center officially began. University president Frank Bolton broke ground and tossed the first shovelful of dirt in a ceremony attended by five thousand students and visitors. Many of the speakers that day used the words "a dream come true" to describe the future student center. Once all the faculty and staff houses located on the designated site were moved, construction on this thoroughly modern building began in earnest. The Robert E. McKee Construction Company of Dallas built the complex, and Robert D. Harrell of Los Angeles served as the decorator. Harrell, well known for his work on the interior of the extravagant Shamrock Hotel in Houston, chose a very stylish yet func-tional décor complementing the contemporary design of the building.[21]

In keeping with the building's mission to serve as a memorial, a bronze plaque listing the names of all Aggies who had given their lives in

The Robert E. McKee Construction Com-pany of Dallas built the MSC in two years at a cost of $1,656,000. Courtesy Cushing Memorial Library and Archives

More than nine hundred Aggies who gave their lives in both world wars are listed on the memorial plaque located at the MSC's original main entrance. Courtesy Cushing Memorial Library and Archives

the world wars was placed at the entrance. Dick Hervey recalls researching every one of the names and writing letters to the parents of those killed. All the work on this sixteen-foot, nine-hundred-pound plaque, from its original design to the final casting, was done on campus by college employees and student workers, with Henry Mooney of the system architect's office designing the plaque. Colonel Willard Chevalier of New York wrote the plaque's inscription, while Gibb Gilchrist came up with the biblical quotation from John 3:15 that appears before the list of more than nine hundred names: "Greater love hath no man than this, that a man lay down his life for his friends." The plaque reads,

In humble reverence this building is dedicated to those men of A&M who gave their lives in defense of our country. Here is enshrined, in spirit and in bronze, enduring tribute to their valor and to their deep devotion. Here their memory shall remain forever fresh—their sacrifices shall not be forgotten.

Gratitude is due those thousands of former students of this college who provided the initial incentive to erect this structure and made liberal contributions to its cost. In their behalf and that of the generous people of Texas as a whole—who made possible its completion—this Center has been created. May it serve as a useful memorial to the heroic sons of A&M who gave their all, enriching the lives of thousands of young Texans now living and others yet unborn.[22]

Everyone on the A&M campus eagerly awaited the completion of the Memorial Student Center, as did the surrounding community. J. T. L. "Lamar" McNew '53 recalls that as a student he gave hundreds of tours, showing off the site to anyone interested in the new structure going up, stepping over holes and onto boards, and pointing out particular details, saying something like, "This is going to be the living room and over there is going to be the bowling alley." He helped them see through the brick and steel, to visualize what it would look like based on the architectural plans, and he told them "what Stark had told me about this broad vision that I didn't completely comprehend."[23] Finally, in September 1950, the student center opened its doors to the students and the public. At a final cost of nearly $2 million to build, the center hosted scores of visitors during a three-day informal opening that offered tours of the building and showcased its plethora of rooms and services. The works of Texas artists and renowned photographers lined the halls, complementing this structure of "unusual beauty and architectural merit."[24]

On Muster, April 21, 1951, the Memorial Student Center was officially dedicated with a colorful, moving ceremony on the front lawn. Tyree

A view of the north side of the newly constructed Memorial Student Center in 1950. Courtesy Memorial Student Center Director's Office

Bell '13, president of the Board of Directors, gave the dedication address, saying that the building was not a typical cold monument but rather a "vibrant living memorial of usefulness." He spoke of the many facilities offered for the students' recreational, cultural, educational, and social life—now all contained under one roof. He talked about how the student center would provide an environment where the "finer aspects of life can enter and influence the rough and ready atmosphere and habits of a man's school."[25] Mrs. E. P. Arneson, of San Antonio, representing A&M's Gold Star families, whose sons had been killed in action, laid a wreath beneath the bronze plaque and eloquently remembered "those beyond sight and touch, who walked here, learned here, laughed here— our sons—are here."[26] The dream had finally come true and a whole new world awaited the young men of A&M. A sleeping giant was about to be awakened on the campus.

TWO

"How Did We Ever Get Along Without It?"

1951–70

WITH THE OPENING OF THE MSC, a new world opened to both cadets and members of the local community, a world featuring luxurious living rooms, formal dining areas, large meeting rooms, a grand ballroom, a first-rate hotel, and a host of other social and recreational amenities. This first air-conditioned building on campus treated students, faculty, and visitors to an environment Tyree Bell aptly described as "so long needed, so long deficient—a social and cultural Center."[1] However, beyond its modern exterior and elegantly decorated interior, MSC director J. Wayne Stark began laying the foundation for exposing Aggies to ideas and concepts not stereotypically associated with A&M and Aggies. Folks rarely used such words as art, international travel, distinguished speakers, and diverse political thought in the same sentence as "Texas A&M" or "Aggie." So while the MSC now served as a central location for student activities and provided much-needed services on what was a very drab campus, Stark also began creating an environment where students' eyes could open to a broader worldview, in terms not only of culture but also in developing leadership. As he explained it, one of the primary missions of the MSC was to "help students learn to live fuller lives after graduation." He wanted the student center to offer a wide spectrum of programs and activities that complemented and

enhanced the formal classroom education. Not only did he perceive the MSC playing the lead role in exposing students to culture but he also saw it as an important vehicle by which to develop leaders. In his mind, the MSC served as a home for student-led committees that would bring diverse programs to the campus and would do so with students gaining a style of leadership training other than the form found inside the military structure of A&M's Corps of Cadets.[2]

Given its crisp new facilities and services, the MSC was quite impressive. Richard R. "Dick" Tumlinson '51 likened the experience to "moving into a new house," with the MSC bringing rich comforts to a rural campus.[3] The student center's design, with its brick and limestone structure, gave the college its first contemporary architecture, with the building surrounded by spacious lawns. Inside, the understated elegance of the MSC also had a "homey" feel, drawing students in to relax, study quietly, meet family and friends, or take a nap on the comfortable furniture along the front hall. As John Whitmore III '51, editor of the *Battalion*, recalled, "You could go off into a corner and study or read, and there were little nooks all over the building."[4] The student center also gave students the opportunity to catch up with world events by reading the Browsing Library's national newspapers (*New York Times, Wall Street Journal*), listening to classical and modern music in the record room, and enjoying some recreational time at the gameroom, bowling alley, or crafts room. The MSC became known as the "living room of the campus," where students could have unlimited refills of coffee, get their mail, and of course, speak to their parents and sweethearts at the telephone center.

The main lounge of the MSC, where students would come to meet parents, girlfriends, and other guests, c. 1951. The stone fireplace, magazines on the coffee tables, and comfortable sofas provided a cozy feel to this lounge area. Courtesy Memorial Student Center Director's Office

The promenade along the front of the MSC, facing Simpson Drill Field, c. 1951. Courtesy Memorial Student Center Director's Office

At first, this telephone center consisted of five booths, with an attendant on duty to staff the switchboard during rush hours. Later, a long line of telephone booths was installed down the narrow hallway by the bowling alley. It was here a homesick "fish" could receive words of encouragement from his parents or a cadet might have the opportunity to catch up with his girl back home. When trainloads and busloads of sweethearts arrived or parents came to visit on campus, there now was a place for

them to stay, with the MSC's sixty-six guest rooms as well as full-service dining facilities to feed them. When such visitors arrived on campus, it was here at the MSC where they received an enthusiastic greeting from the passionate, legendary Pinckney L. "Pinkie" Downs '06 (1906), Texas A&M's official greeter. Usually sporting a tie, an old hat, and always a smile, Pinkie typically staffed the student center's front door or roamed throughout the building, shaking hands and telling stories. Robert L. "Bob" Walker '58 remembers most people saying, "If you ever want to find Pinkie, he'll be at the MSC."[5]

While having the enormous task of managing the new facility, Wayne Stark put into practice his vision of student programs. Stark structured the MSC organization even before the building opened by first establishing a governing body, which he believed actively put "citizenship and self-government into practice in the Student Center." This governing body, the MSC Council, comprised the main groups using the student center—students, former students, and faculty. The MSC Council initially consisted of eight students, five faculty members, two former students, and the director of the MSC. The council formulated general policies for the MSC and supervised the planning and operation of the activities and events within the center. When it first convened in the spring of 1950, the MSC Council consisted of Dr. J. H. Quisenberry '31, Dr. W. H. Delaplane, Phil Goode '38, C. A. Roeber, John Rowlett, Dick Hervey '42, Sid Loveless '38, H. W. Beutel '50, Hal Stringer '50, Joe Fuller

'49 (first MSC Council president), Lavon Massengale Jr. '51, Dick Ingels '52, Dan Davis '52, Lamar McNew Jr. '53, and Joe Wallace '53, along with Stark. The first order of business for the council included the creation of a constitution and by-laws for the government of the MSC. The constitution called for the selection of a president and vice president—both student positions elected by members of the council. The constitution also called for the creation of the MSC Directorate, a body directly under the MSC Council in the student center's organization that consisted of the chairmen and presidents of the various MSC committees and clubs. Their job included planning the social and educational programs, allocating room for displays, estimating budgets for programs, and generally ensuring cooperation between the various committees.[6]

Neither the MSC Council nor the MSC Directorate handled any of the student center's business affairs dealing with the food department, the guest rooms, the gift shop, the bowling alley, or the barbershop. The policies and procedures for those departments fell under the sole management of the MSC director. Stark organized the MSC business operations and service centers by creating two separate divisions, each comprising professional staff. C. F. Gent, assistant director and business manager, headed the business division, which handled services such as the guest rooms, food operations, banquet rooms, gift shop, barbershop, and the telephone center. Mozelle Holland served as the acting manager of the guest rooms, in charge of managing reservations requests

One of the early MSC Councils, which included Dr. John H. Quisenberry, David L. Coslett, Joe R. Fuller, R. A. "Dick" Ingels, Dan W. Davis, Dick Hervey, Lamar McNew Jr., F. E. Smith, Sidney L. Loveless, Dr. W. H. Delaplane, C. A. Roeber, J. M. Rowlett, J. Wayne Stark, Clayton L. Selph, Joe Wallace, L. V. Massengale, and Ferris Brown. Photo from *Aggieland,* 1951

and overseeing the housekeeping staff. Margaret Sartor worked as the MSC food director, having come to College Station after a notable career supervising the food operations that fed twelve hundred people a day at Hermann Hospital in Houston. The other division, the social and educational department, managed the MSC Browsing Library, the art programs, the craft shop, record room, and dance areas. Ann Hilliard supervised this department and also worked closely with the MSC student-led committees, "not telling them what to do . . . they will choose their own activities and I will give them advice and aid in organizing their clubs and groups." Helen Atterbury worked as Stark's dedicated secretary, always striving to keep up with his fast pace and ever-broadening vision for the MSC.[7]

As for the setting of policies on the everyday use of the MSC, what remains unclear is whether or not the MSC Council was the first to formally designate the grass surrounding the MSC as a memorial. In fact, this well-respected tradition, and the signage added later to caution visitors not to walk on any of the grass surrounding the MSC, is clouded in mystery as to its origin. Several Aggies interviewed for this book say the tradition began immediately upon the MSC's opening. Others have no recollection of when the tradition started but do remember it was customary for cadets in uniform never to walk on the grass anyway. Still, some staff at the MSC recall Wayne Stark telling the story about how blueprints for the MSC contained the word "memorial" at all the outside corners of the building, thus giving the impression the entire grass area surrounding the building had somehow been designated as a memorial. Even photos from the dedication ceremony for the MSC and Muster on April 21, 1951, show some people sitting on the front lawn of the building as well as the Ross Volunteers standing on the grass to fire a twenty-one-gun salute. Yet it was not until May 1953 that the MSC Council passed the motion for a policy stating that "the grass and landscape areas adjacent to the MSC [shall] not be used for any type of mass meetings, except with the specific approval of the Council."[8]

While much Aggie folklore remains as to the beginnings of this tradition, its spirit has endured throughout the MSC's history—to respect and honor those Aggies who died in war. An additional way to honor them did officially originate in 1953 with the adoption of the hats-off policy. Although many members of the student body instinctively removed their hats as they entered the MSC, it was brought to the MSC Council's attention that visitors and guests did not always do so. After much discussion, the council adopted the following policy in November 1953: "Since the Memorial Student Center is a memorial to those men of Texas A&M who gave their lives during World War I and War II, it shall be requested of all gentlemen entering the building to remove their hats while in any section of the Union building." The council requested that the staff of the MSC help in establishing this custom, and it provided copies to the Corps and other organizations, asking for their assistance implementing the policy. Still today, before entering the MSC, it is customary for a male to remove his hat as a sign of respect for these fallen former students, and it is often common to hear students politely ask visitors to "uncover." To further honor Aggie war heroes, upon the recommendation of A&M president Frank Bolton the student center became the permanent home for the pictures and citations of the seven former students who received the Medal of Honor. These seven Aggies—Major Horace S. Carswell, Jr. '38, Lieutenant Thomas W. Fowler '43, Sergeant William G. Harrell '43, Lieutenant Lloyd H. Hughes '43, Sergeant George D. Keathley '37, Lieutenant Turney W. Leonard '42, and Lieutenant Eli L. Whiteley '41—are memorialized with plaques that include their picture, their medal, and a written account of their heroic efforts. Cadets and guests alike are reminded of their bravery and sacrifice when they visit the MSC, and today these plaques rest on the columns of the north hallway looking out onto Simpson Drill Field.[9]

The first committees of the MSC included the Art Gallery Committee, Browsing Library Committee, Camera Club, Dance Committee, Games Committee, Music Committee, and the House Committee. These committees were extremely busy when the MSC opened, providing numerous

Ross Volunteers standing on the grass outside the front entrance of the MSC during its dedication on April 21, 1951. In 1953, the MSC Council voted that the grass and landscape adjacent to the student center would not be used for any type of mass meetings, except on the specific approval of the council. Courtesy Cushing Memorial Library and Archives

programs and activities for the A&M campus, the likes of which had not been seen before at the college. In the year the MSC opened, exhibits by the Art Gallery Committee and the Camera Club brought art to the "everyday life" of the A&M student body, the Music Committee brought Maria de León-Ortega from Mexico City for a program on Latin American music, and the Dance Committee sponsored eight dances in its first year, as well as having five hundred students participate in dance classes. In his first annual report to the A&M president, Stark pointed out that in terms of its facilities and services, the MSC served well as the college's showplace during important functions that year, particularly when General Dwight Eisenhower attended President M. T. Harrington's inauguration. He additionally reported that nearly 1 million people were served in the dining room and other food service areas, 22,500 people used the guest rooms, and more than 100,000 people used the bowling alley and the barbershop in the MSC's first year of operation. He commented that time and time again he heard people who came through the MSC ask, "How did we ever get along without it?"[10]

To help students learn more about the weekly offerings at the student center, the *MSC Radio Show,* broadcast on A&M's WTAW, featured announcements about committee activities, a newscast, and classical music. Don Friend '55 was the broadcaster in 1952, and in 1953, Charles Parker '55, who became MSC Council president in 1954–1955, awakened students every morning with his "Coffee Club" program. Known as the

General Dwight D. Eisenhower, shown attending the inauguration for A&M president M. T. Harrington in 1951, was one of the first dignitaries to visit the new Memorial Student Center. Courtesy Cushing Memorial Library and Archives

"Old D. J.," Parker could be heard percolating coffee in the background while he did his program, which featured music ranging from the Fred Waring orchestra to hit tunes from artists such as Billy May. Later on, Parker became convinced the MSC should have a committee charged with bringing television to the campus. So, with encouragement from Stark, Parker remembers "soliciting alumni because we needed to raise ten thousand dollars to get it running," and he ultimately set up a television set in the MSC lobby.[11]

Over the next few years, the MSC offered social and cultural experiences many Aggies had never encountered but that, given the opportunity, they became very willing to participate in and learn about. Stark stressed the importance of good manners and expected them from the students. He would boldly criticize a student's personal habits if needed, telling him to "sit up straight," "get a haircut," or "stop putting your hand in front of your mouth."[12] So, given the rough-edged nature of A&M and many of its rural students, Stark created etiquette classes, taught by Ann Hilliard, in which students learned about the niceties of society, including proper table manners. The Dance Committee also started Café Rue Pinalle in 1952, using one of the basement rooms of the MSC as sort of a "nightclub" without the alcoholic beverages. There might be a cabaret act or band playing, and as Herbert W. "Bud" Whitney '56 (sixth MSC Council president) recalls, it was a "nice place to take a date" since there were no such establishments on campus and very

The MSC Dance Committee's version of a French cabaret, called "Café Rue Pinalle," had its grand opening in the bowling area of the student center on February 15, 1952. For fifty cents per person, one could enjoy dancing, soft drinks, and sandwiches. Large murals of French night life decorated the area, and it was an extremely popular place to take a date. Courtesy Cushing Memorial Library and Archives

few in College Station and Bryan.[13] To expose A&M students to more famous visual arts, Stark worked with the Art Gallery Committee in 1953 to bring in an exhibit of famous European and American paintings valued at half a million dollars. For two weeks, students and members of the college community, as well as public school students, could browse the featured works by Renoir, Pissarro, Monet, and Winslow Homer. The MSC also displayed an exhibit of famous Vincent van Gogh paintings from a private collection.[14]

Another unique collection found a permanent home on the second floor of the MSC—the Metzger Gun Collection. In 1949, Carl Metzger gave A&M his personal collection of more than four hundred hand and shoulder weapons as well as firearm accessories. It had lain buried in storage until the MSC opened. This collection displayed weapons representing various time periods in American and Texas history.[15]

In 1953, Stark saw the need for a committee that could host renowned speakers, bringing them and their various viewpoints to the insulated A&M campus. He founded the MSC Great Issues Committee for the purpose of presenting speakers and programs that would address social and economic issues of local, state, national, and international interest. Over the next ten years, this committee brought distinguished speakers such as Supreme Court Justice Tom C. Clark, Assistant Secretary of Defense Carter L. Burgess, Will Rogers Jr., Dr. Edward Teller (father of the hydrogen bomb), Robert F. Kennedy, and even a few controversial figures such as labor leader James B. Carey, vice president of the AFL-CIO. Interestingly, Stark had Representative Olin E. "Tiger" Teague '32 investigate Carey's background given the concerns of Dr. D. W. Williams, A&M's acting president, that "there are going to be objections to the Labor Leader as a speaker on our campus." Stark provided Williams with his findings, and Carey spoke at the Great Issues event, although the president forewarned, "While I have no enthusiasm for Mr. Carey, I do not see any reason why he should not speak on campus. . . . I do think that you should recognize that there will be criticism and be prepared to meet it."[16]

Stark also believed the MSC could further develop the leadership skills of A&M students in a way much different from what the Corps of Cadets currently offered. Students who became active in the MSC's governmental structure as well as its programs found the experience greatly enriched their leadership development as well as their personal growth. As Stark wrote in 1948 in a memo to E. L. Angell, assistant to the A&M president, "The union is a laboratory of student management and self-expression." It is doubtful, given A&M's military culture at the time, that self-expression was a characteristic encouraged wholeheartedly by the administration and Corps leadership. Yet Stark believed that his vision for the MSC, both in terms of student development and programming, could supplement the Corps experience in order to make A&M students more well-rounded individuals. The Corps spirit and culture already provided a solid foundation of leadership development that Stark believed he could further build upon to enhance students' college experience. Perhaps having this overall leadership culture and tradition in place at A&M since its inception is what made students so receptive to participating in MSC programs and enhanced their desire to pursue leadership positions within the organization. It is no coincidence that the vast majority of MSC Council and MSC Directorate members also held officer positions within the Corps.[17]

For those not in the Corps, the MSC provided a welcome opportunity to become active and assume campus leadership roles on a much broader scale than what was previously available at the college. When the veterans of World War II returned to A&M to pursue their GI Bill–sponsored education, the Corps of Cadets structure, in place for more than seventy years, held little attraction for them. These incoming students had experienced war firsthand and had no desire to don a cadet uniform. For the first time in the college's history, there were large numbers of students not in uniform and not part of the Corps. Some tensions occasionally surfaced between the veterans and the cadets, but all in all, the mix of students got along with one another. However, beginning in the mid-1940s and well into the mid-1950s, discussion brewed among A&M administrators, legislators, and former students as to the future direction of Texas A&M—how to further expand enrollment and the scope of programs offered on campus in an ever-changing, advancing society. The controversial question about making the Corps noncompulsory came under fierce debate, and in the fall of 1954, membership in the Corps became optional (a decision reversed in November 1957). The MSC was at the right place at the right time to take advantage of this transition occurring on campus. There were now numerous students who were not part of the Corps but were searching for ways to become involved in the university and, in many cases, to become leaders on campus. Stark knew just where to lead them—to the MSC. A student could join a committee, gain practical experience planning a program or an exhibit, and then be encouraged to interview for a leadership position on the MSC Council or Directorate.[18]

In 1953, MSC Council president John S. Samuels III '54 organized a leadership conference at the student center to further facilitate a better working relationship between cadets and noncadets represented within the MSC structure, as well as other student leaders across campus who were involved in the MSC. He saw the need to bring everyone together so they could frankly discuss the role of the MSC within the confines of a very conservative A&M structure. This conference may have been presented by Wayne Stark to the university administration as a program to develop leaders (later on it would evolve into an annual retreat known as the MSC Fall Leadership Conference), but as Samuels recalls, it was more about giving students the opportunity to express and reflect on the various issues facing A&M and have them brainstorm on the role the MSC should play through its programs, speakers, and exhibits. These students, several of whom also held editorial positions at the *Battalion,* often questioned the hard-core, traditional military views represented by the administration. In one instance, the administration shut down the school newspaper for a short time in the early 1950s. Now, the MSC provided an outlet for students to consider wide-ranging worldviews and cultures—giving them the opportunity to sponsor programs with perhaps a more controversial speaker or showcasing a diverse cultural exhibit never seen before on the campus. Of course, these programs or exhibits sometimes did not sit too well with the college administration. On several occasions, Stark and the MSC Arts Committee attempted to bring art exhibitions that included images of nudes. Samuels remembers one instance in which he, Stark, and committee members were hanging up the exhibit and President Tom Harrington walked by. He immediately ordered them to remove the paintings and sketches. Samuels recalls that Stark was "taken aback" but said he would take them down. However, Samuels noticed two days later that they were put back up.[19]

Yet MSC programs and the unique leadership development opportunities they offered did not appeal just to the "non-regs" (non-regulation, that is, students who were not members of the Corps). Naturally, cadets were very involved in the MSC and its leadership structure since total enrollment at A&M averaged 7,136 from 1955 to 1959, with the Corps enrollment averaging 3,900 cadets during that time. The MSC, just by the nature of its facilities alone, provided a wonderful refuge for those who wanted a brief escape from military life. John Whitmore '51 recalls thinking, "When somebody found his way to the MSC, he would not want to come out," particularly since it informally served as a haven from the class-hierarchy atmosphere of the Corps.[20] Given the MSC's purpose to give all students a place for spending their leisure time, it made sense that underclassmen were not to be harassed within the walls of this memorial. However, in the earliest days of the MSC, the *Battalion* reported occurrences of freshmen being hazed or told that using the MSC was a privilege reserved for upperclassmen. In an effort to counter the latter claim, the MSC Council sponsored an open house for incoming freshmen in 1953, displaying exhibits from every MSC committee and encouraging newcomers to get involved. So, with its student-led programs, the MSC functioned as the only entity on campus in which

In 1953, the student center hosted one of its first open house programs, with the theme, "Get acquainted with your MSC." Young women from the local community acted as hostesses while the various MSC committees set up exhibits showcasing their programs. The "Café Rue Pinalle" exhibit is especially noteworthy for its "Girls, girls, girls" sign, visible in the background on the right. Courtesy Memorial Student Center Director's Office

all students—cadets and "non-regs"—could explore new ideas, discover culture, take a risk producing a program, or even question the status quo. Stark believed "a visit [to the MSC] for one activity, say a 'Coke' in the fountain area, will expose the students to, and perhaps inspire some of them to engage in another activity—say an art exhibit; thus we have a blending of cultural interest and daily living—blending together into an art in living." This was the setting nurtured by Stark, one where students could learn more about citizenship, leadership, and the broader world that existed outside rural College Station.[21]

Whether it be for a cadet or a "non-reg" student, when Stark saw the opportunity for a leadership training moment, he avidly pursued it. One example of how he challenged students to bring out their leadership potential is illustrated with the birth of one of the MSC's most distinguished programs—SCONA, the Student Conference on National Affairs. In January 1955, MSC president Bud Whitney '56 returned to the A&M campus after attending West Point's SCUSA (Student Conference on U.S. Affairs) program. This conference thoroughly impressed Whitney, who discussed his experience with Stark and other MSC students. Stark then encouraged Whitney to put on a similar program at A&M. Whitney recruited John W. Jenkins '56 to be the chairman of the conference, but Stark made it perfectly clear he was not going to coordinate this event. Whitney and Jenkins recall Stark saying, "I'm not going to set this thing up. I want you guys to set this up. I'll get you phone numbers and maybe some contacts, but you have to go make the contacts and raise the money." With his encouragement, the two traveled the roads of Texas in Jenkins's family car during the spring and summer of 1955 trying to secure speakers and raise twelve thousand dollars for the event's budget. At one point, they even burned up the Mercury's engine in pursuit of funding. Lamar Fleming Jr., chairman of the board for Anderson Clayton, actually furnished the young men with an office in the company's suite to use whenever they came to Houston. After meeting with numerous folks, they raised the twelve thousand dollars and began planning the first conference, which dealt with the role of the United States in world affairs. Keynote speakers for that first conference included Fleming and George C. McGhee, a former assistant secretary of state. Other distinguished speakers included General William J. Donovan, head of the Office of Strategic Services during World War II (the OSS was the predecessor agency to the CIA), and Thruston B. Morton, assistant secretary of state. More than one hundred students from thirteen states, Mexico, and Canada attended, making the conference extraordinarily successful.[22]

A tradition was born, and SCONA continued to bring distinguished speakers, state dignitaries, and a diverse host of college students to the

The founders of SCONA, Herbert "Bud" Whitney and John W. Jenkins, talking to Lamar Fleming Jr., chairman of the board for Anderson Clayton and Company, who was one of the keynote speakers at SCONA I in 1955. Left to right: Fleming, Jenkins, Jack Lunsford, A&M president D. H. Morgan, and Whitney. U.S. Representative Olin E. "Tiger" Teague is standing in the center. Courtesy Memorial Student Center Director's Office

little town of College Station. In fact, the first African American allowed to spend the night in the MSC guest rooms was a SCONA delegate from Texas A&I University–Kingsville. Vance Shaw, now a retired colonel of the U.S. Air Force, was a student leader at Texas A&I and was chosen as one of the university's representatives to SCONA in 1962. However, not long after the invitation, he was told he could not participate because he was African American and A&M was not an integrated campus. Later, he received word that he could attend the conference but would not be allowed to stay in the MSC guest rooms along with all the other SCONA delegates. Instead, he would stay at the home of an African American family in Hearne, nearly thirty miles away. Texas A&I's underground newspaper uncovered the story and somehow managed to bring the issue to Vice President Lyndon B. Johnson's attention. Johnson spoke at SCONA II in 1956 as a senator and was returning as keynote speaker for the 1962 SCONA. According to Shaw, Johnson interceded and the next thing he knew, he attended SCONA and shared a guest room at the MSC with a delegate from the Naval Academy. MSC president James E. Ray '62 served as his escort, and as Shaw remembers, he and Ray sat on the very first row during Johnson's keynote address. At the conclusion of his

Senator Lyndon B. Johnson speaking at SCONA II in 1956. He came to campus numerous times to participate in MSC Great Issues and other presentations, including serving as the keynote speaker for SCONA VIII in 1962 when he was vice president.
Courtesy MSC SCONA historical files

speech, Johnson came down to the first row and greeted Shaw, asking, "How are they treating you?" Shaw replied, "Just fine, sir." Shaw was the only African American SCONA delegate that year, but he recalls the Aggies being very friendly and sociable toward him. Today, he still has a deep affection for Texas A&M and the many friends he made there.[23]

SCONA gave Aggies the opportunity to dream big, and in the process, they landed some impressive speakers. Of course, Johnson served as the keynote speaker in 1956 and again in 1962. Senator Hubert Humphrey participated in SCONA III after a group of student committee leaders visited him at the Shamrock Hotel in Houston, persuading him to speak at the conference. John H. Lindsey '44 recalls Stark informed him that Hubert Humphrey had originally agreed to speak at the conference but then reconsidered because of a prior commitment. Lindsey mentioned to Stark that the senator was in Houston for a speaking engagement. Stark encouraged three SCONA students to ride with Lindsey back to Houston, where the three students called Humphrey from the Shamrock's lobby telephone and were able to persuade his aide to allow them to come up and meet with the senator. While Lindsey waited downstairs, the students visited with Humphrey and he ultimately agreed to be one of the keynote speakers for SCONA III. Lindsey recalls thinking to himself, "What am I doing here?" Over time, this pattern of persuading a former student to help current students with MSC endeavors became Stark's hallmark modus operandi.[24]

Perhaps no one in A&M's history developed as large or as intricate a former student network as Wayne Stark did. Although no one really knows how it began, Stark made it a point to meet and remain in contact with significant numbers of former students, and he used these connections beginning in the early days of the MSC. He stayed in touch with numerous Aggies in business, law, and even politics, such as U.S. Representative Olin Teague '32, working his network to get funding and speakers for various MSC programs. Stark kept extensive files on every former student he met, compiling meticulous notes from conversations and maintaining diligent correspondence. He had an amazing memory for details and could often recall former students' intricate family and business connections. Stark became good friends with a former student named Dr. Larry Fouraker '47, and this relationship resulted in something inconceivable for A&M students of the time—Aggies getting their graduate degrees at Harvard.

Stark's relationship with Fouraker is of great importance because this friendship yielded long-term, immeasurable benefits to A&M students and the university—first, by creating a direct pipeline of Aggies going to Harvard Business School, where they gained insight into culture and business practices outside the small-town Texas scene, and secondly, by creating highly successful former students who would go on to provide significant volunteer support and financial contributions to Texas A&M. Fouraker joined the faculty at Harvard Business School in 1961 and served as dean from 1970 to 1980. As early as the 1950s, Stark's vision of Aggies going beyond the state's borders and experiencing the world naturally led him to believe many opportunities awaited these young men at the best graduate schools in the country. He was very skillful at planting the notion of obtaining a graduate degree in those he viewed as having the right qualities to succeed in prestigious graduate programs. It did not matter to him whether or not a young man had ever traveled outside of his hometown, College Station, or farther north than Dallas. When Stark saw a student who exhibited leadership potential and whom he thought would do well, he persistently encouraged him to pursue a law degree or a master's in business administration. Stark viewed Harvard Business School as the most prestigious program, and so it was there that Aggies should go and make their mark. He used his connection with Fouraker to make that happen. John Jenkins '56 recalls Stark pushed him to consider going to Harvard (he ultimately did attend), but he had to first fulfill his air force duty. After getting out of the air force, Jenkins called Stark to inform him he was now ready to go to business school. Stark responded by saying, "It's about time you finally decided to do it. What did you wait so long for?" Jenkins filled out the Harvard application quickly, accompanied by the infallible Stark recommendation, and sent one to Stanford as well, per Stark's strict instructions of always having a "backup" choice.[25]

By the early 1960s, other former MSC leaders headed up to Boston-Cambridge as Stark cultivated his relationship with Fouraker and laid the foundation for what would become an amazing former student network within the ivy-covered walls of Harvard. Those Harvard-bound Aggies included John Samuels '54 (Harvard Law School), Charles Parker '55 (Harvard Business School), Jon L. Hagler '58 (Harvard Business School), Don Cloud '59 (Harvard Business School), William B. "Bill" Heye '60 (Harvard Business School), Robert Hall '63 (Harvard Business School), E. Lee Walker '64 (Harvard Business School), Hector Gutierrez Jr. '69 (Harvard Business School), and numerous other Aggies. Stark always arranged for former A&M students at Harvard to host potential Aggie graduate students, showing them around the campus and filling them in on what graduate school would be like. However, one did not even have to be active in MSC organizations for Stark to single out a student whom he thought would do well in graduate school. E. Lee Walker, a star basketball player and also president of the A&M Russian Club, met Stark when he came to the MSC to inquire about finding Russian films on campus. He recalls Stark took great interest in him, especially since he was from the small town of Three Rivers and was a good student majoring in physics. From their initial meeting, Walker remembers, "I was kind of grist for his mill," and he was tenaciously encouraged to apply to Harvard Business School.[26] Stark had this uncanny ability to take a boy from a small town who was majoring in engineering, agriculture, or some other technical degree and put thoughts and dreams into his head that were far beyond his wildest imagination. Jon

Students reading and studying in the MSC Browsing Library. Director J. Wayne Stark always made sure there were copies of the New York Times, Wall Street Journal, *and other national newspapers available so Aggies could be exposed to the world outside of Aggieland, their hometowns, and Texas.* Courtesy Memorial Student Center Director's Office

Hagler echoes the sentiments of many grateful Aggies when he says, "I'm sure I never would have gone to Harvard Business School if it hadn't been for Wayne."[27]

In conjunction with his vision to see Aggies become leaders in business, industry, and law, Stark exposed students to the possibility of careers in those fields by forming the MSC MBA/Law Committee in the late 1960s. Its purpose was to break the traditional assumptions associated with these professions, such as the idea that one had to attain a specific undergraduate degree to succeed in these graduate programs. Stark invited engineering students, geosciences students, and students from nontraditional majors to consider an advanced degree in law or business, encouraging them to become a part of this unique MSC committee. The committee offered programs bringing guest speakers and representatives from various graduate business and law schools to meet with interested students. Also, Stark used this opportunity to bring back to campus successful former students who had careers in business and law so that they could interact with students.[28]

While working to send Aggies out of Texas to broaden their experiences, Stark also focused on bringing national attention back to Texas A&M and the MSC. As early as 1949, Stark became active in the Association of College Unions–International (ACU-I), hosting regional meetings on the A&M campus even before the MSC was actually built. He met regularly with his counterparts at other universities and took every opportunity to bring them to College Station to show off the MSC's facilities and student programs. He also encouraged student participation in this organization, and during the 1951–52 school year, John Samuels '54 became the student president of the ACU-I. In 1957–58, MSC president Don McGinty '58 became the president of the region 9 ACU-I board, while Stark served as the president of the entire organization. By the 1960s, the MSC rose in the ranks of student unions, gaining a reputation as one of the premier student centers in the country, given its physical size, its quality facilities and services, and its unique role in student programming and leadership development. Programs such as SCONA and Great Issues garnered even more recognition for the MSC and A&M as a whole. These specific programs created the opportunity for high-profile speakers to visit A&M for the first time in many cases. National politicians, distinguished scientists, lawyers, journalists, and lecturers such as Wernher von Braun, Dr. Edward Teller, and of course Lyndon B. Johnson, Robert Kennedy, and Hubert Humphrey all spoke to Aggies through various MSC programs. For the first time in its history, A&M began establishing a name for itself through programs outside the Corps of Cadets and the military field.[29]

As Texas A&M entered the 1960s, no one could have guessed the magnitude of changes that would occur at the college or the sweeping cultural shifts in America. Americans rushed into an age filled with Elvis, the Beatles, color TV, John F. Kennedy, the cold war, Martin Luther King, Woodstock, hippies, integration, and the Vietnam War. Many college campuses became the settings for protests against the "Establishment" and against the war in Vietnam. Groups such as Students for a Democratic Society (SDS) established chapters at more than three hundred campuses and organized hostile demonstrations, particularly to oppose the Vietnam War and the presence of ROTC programs. Given its ultraconservative student body and military image, A&M never experienced the volatile flare-ups found at other college campuses but did face the challenge of how to cope with the national atmosphere and political climate. When James Earl Rudder became A&M president in 1959, A&M's student body numbered 7,094, with 3,803 of those students being in the Corps. He inherited a college at an important crossroads—fighting to hold on to its fundamental, traditional roots and military heritage while trying to lay out a path for its image and growth in the modern age. Rudder recognized that A&M might have to make some changes in order to remain relevant in a rapidly shifting society, yet he felt the college could do so while still staying true to core Aggie values and ideals. After broad analysis through the *Aspirations Study,* the *Century Study,* and the *Blueprint for Progress,* the administration adopted several recommendations that would have a dramatic impact on the A&M campus. The longstanding issue of coeducation, promoted for years by state senator Bill Moore '40 and others, finally got settled in the spring of 1963, when the Board of Directors approved a plan to admit women on a "limited" basis. That same year, the formal name of the college changed from the Agricultural and Mechanical College of Texas to Texas A&M University. In 1965, the Board of Directors eliminated compulsory enrollment in the Corps of Cadets for entering freshmen.[30]

J. Wayne Stark long believed the MSC could be the leader in bringing challenging issues and diverse programs to a campus historically embracing only traditional, conservative, military-focused views. He saw this as the duty of the "other education"—one that would expose students to a wide range of culture and thought. Stark wanted to arm Aggies with a broader knowledge and perspective so they could be successful in an ever-changing world. So, it comes with no surprise that while the university administration wrestled with how to meet the challenges of the 1960s, Stark and the MSC Council were busy creating committees to deal with the recent changes in the world, the nation, and the community. In 1966, the council created the Political Forum Committee as an outlet for political debate and discussion on the hot topics of the day. Candidates from all parties came to speak to the students at these programs. The committee also sponsored panel discussions on political issues important to the United States and the world, bringing in diverse viewpoints.

When African American students began enrolling at A&M, the MSC stepped in to meet the needs of this new student demographic. Back in 1963, the A&M Board of Directors had approved racial integration, and three African Americans enrolled for the first summer session—Vernell Jackson, Leroy Sterling, and George D. Sutton. In the spring of 1968, James L. Courtney '67 became the first African American undergraduate student to graduate from A&M. By 1969, A&M officials had attempted to form the ad hoc Committee on Black Student Affairs as a way of bringing African American students together with civilian students and representatives of

The MSC Black Awareness Committee was formed in 1970 to bring cultural awareness of the African American heritage to A&M as well as provide a forum in which African American students could integrate into campus life. This photo shows some of the first members of the committee. Photo from *Aggieland,* 1972

the Corps, providing a forum for the discussion of issues important to African American students. However, African American students never felt a sense of ownership of this committee and looked for other ways to get a recognized committee on campus. Thomas C. Fitzhugh III, MSC president from 1970 to 1971, recalls that as more African American students came to A&M, Stark fervently believed the campus needed an MSC committee for African American students. He envisioned a group integrating the students into campus life and also providing the opportunity for them to expose A&M to their culture. In 1970, the MSC Council took the lead and created a new committee called the Black Awareness Committee (BAC). Its purpose involved providing leadership skills to students through planning and implementing quality cultural programs such as bringing speakers to campus and hosting dances and art exhibits, all of which would enhance the multicultural experience of the university community and create a better understanding of African American heritage and culture. Shelton Wallace '71, the first BAC chairman, agreed that by expressing their culture and "by feeling a part of A&M, black students could feel more at ease in a predominantly white institution." He acknowledged that "since we live together, work together, and go to school together, we should learn about each other, . . . and we now have an element with which to do this."[31]

In the 1960s, the MSC was growing in terms of student-sponsored programs and to a large extent was beginning to outgrow its physical space with so many campus activities and organizations finding a home inside the building. In terms of facilities, most of the functions and activities once held at the YMCA Building were now being completely absorbed by the MSC, and the "Y" met its fate of being converted to much-needed office space for different university departments. The Aggieland Inn, which had closed its kitchen and dining room in 1950, held on to its hotel rooms for a little while longer to help with overflow at the MSC guest rooms. Yet, in 1955, this use was discontinued and the building was finally razed in 1965. The entertainment series, Town Hall, which originally started as a committee in the Student Life Department, came under the auspices of the MSC and continued securing popular musical artists and groups to play on the A&M campus, some examples being the Fifth Dimension, Simon and Garfunkel, Paul Revere and the Raiders, the Association, and the Johnny Mathis show. Robert F. Gonzales '68, chair of the committee in 1967–1968, recalls that Town Hall brought nineteen shows to the A&M campus through its four series—Town Hall Series, Town Hall Extra, Rotary Community Series (predecessor to the current MSC Opera and Performing Arts Society), and the Artist Showcase Series.[32]

Always with a focus on broadening the cultural horizons of Aggie students, the Arts Committee continued to bring art exhibits and lectures to campus. The MSC Travel Committee also gained momentum, particularly in terms of international travel, by taking a group charter flight to London in 1966. Other excursions followed, including ski trips to Switzerland and France. Of course, Stark always saw the value in getting Aggies to travel overseas, and in 1959, he became A&M's sponsor for the national Experiment in International Living program. This three- to five-week summer exchange program immersed participants in the daily life of another culture and included countries in Europe, Asia, Africa, and the Americas. Stark constantly encouraged students to participate in this program and concocted unique ways of finding funding

Aggies relaxing in the Alps (c. 1970) during one of the many ski trips taken by the MSC Travel Committee. Courtesy Memorial Student Center Director's Office

for cash-strapped students to participate in any type of foreign travel experience. He often called upon former students to help fund trips, work out employment opportunities, or arrange creative transportation options for students. Lee Walker '64 recalls going to Yugoslavia through the Experiment in International Living, the "sort of thing which would never occur to someone from Three Rivers, Texas." Another year, Walker led a group of students to Sweden. Later, as a student at Harvard Business School, he recalls needing to find a summer job to help pay his loans and other expenses. Stark, however, emphatically believed Walker should go to Africa for the summer and worked out a unique scenario for him to get there. If Walker could hitchhike to Newport News by a certain date, Stark could arrange for him to work on a coal freighter. Once he got to Europe, he was to go to Geneva and apply for a job working for Esso Africa. Stark had worked all the details out with George Comnas '35, who was the president of Esso Africa.[33]

Likewise, Patrick G. "Pat" Rehmet '68, deputy Corps commander in 1967–68 and a leader in SCONA, remembers Stark calling him into his office to sit on the "infamous green couch" where he worked to persuade Rehmet to travel overseas through the Experiment in International Living program.[34] Rehmet knew his family did not have the money for such an experience, but Stark told him, "You get permission and I'll get the money." He recalls Stark phoning three former students, and in three days, he had the funds and Rehmet was on his way to Poland and the Soviet Union. Hector Gutierrez '69, A&M's first Hispanic Corps commander, also went to Poland and the Soviet Union through the program, and he credited Stark with instilling in him "the curiosity for learning about other countries and other people." Gutierrez, Rehmet, and Walker are just a few of the many beneficiaries of the amazing Stark network.[35]

Within the walls of the MSC, Stark and the MSC Council continued to plan cultural travel experiences for Aggies a bit closer to home. In 1963, Stark, former student John Lindsey '44, and MSC president James Ray '63 began the Texas A&M Student Leadership Training Program, taking twenty student leaders to Houston for a weekend. Later called the MSC Spring Leadership Trip, this program exposed A&M students to the cultural aspects of society by having them visit museums, attend symphonies and plays, and dine at fine restaurants. Lindsey and some other former students hosted the students and made all the arrangements with the various venues. Some of the first trips were to Houston, where students could visit NASA's Manned Space Center, see a play at the Alley Theatre, have dinner at the Shamrock Hotel, take a tour of the Museum of Fine Arts, and attend performances by the Houston Symphony and the Houston Ballet. Most Aggies had never been to a major symphony or dined at fine restaurants, so having this opportunity was quite an eye-opening experience. Bill Carter '69, president of the A&M Student Senate in 1968–1969, remembers the exposure as being terrific but also recognized that "Stark was trying to tell us, when you get out in business, you are going to go to cocktail parties, you are going to go to the theatre, you are going to go to the symphony . . . you need to know how to behave and how to act—what to do and what not to do!" An experience like this, sponsored by an A&M entity, exemplifies the broad changes sweeping through A&M in the 1960s.[36]

Wayne Stark himself was a living example of these transformative changes—coming from a rural background but now espousing the virtues of cultural awareness, international travel, graduate school, and leadership development. No one knows for sure when he first recognized the importance of these experiences for young Aggies, because he was neither an art connoisseur nor a world traveler, but most agree that he was extremely zealous, often overbearing, in trying to convey their importance to students. Bill Heye '60, Corps commander in 1959–60, acknowledges that Stark pushed him hard when he was traveling for job interviews during his upperclass years, telling him not to worry so much about the job prospects but rather to concentrate on cultural opportunities. He advised the young man, "Find the opera—you should attend. You should go to this museum or that museum."[37] Students saw Stark's tenacity as quite intimidating but learned quickly of his complete devotion to the development of students—caring for them, giving them sound advice, and encouraging them to dream big dreams. Many students remember spending time in Stark's office, sitting on the legendary green couch—sinking into its cushions as Stark went on and on about the importance of going to graduate school and intermittently talked on the phone with former students. Robert Gonzales '68 always tried to conduct business with Stark while standing up because "I knew if I sat down on the couch, I was locked in for at least an hour!"[38]

On other occasions, the green couch was not the place one wanted to find oneself. Frank Muller '65, student body president for 1964–65, recalls the ability of Stark "to spank you with words; he had an ability to make you feel a half an inch tall . . . there was no excuse that ever worked with him. J. Wayne looked for one thing and that was excellence, and he made you explain—sometimes in writing, but mostly on the green couch—why you didn't give 110 percent."[39] Ruth Hewitt, Stark's secretary during this period and his "right-hand person," usually provided a sympathetic ear and shoulder for those who found themselves on the receiving end of a Wayne Stark lecture. Many students, such as Hector Gutierrez, Robert Gonzales, and numerous others regarded her as their "second mom," hanging out at her home with her family, including her son, Tommy Hewitt '72. Of course, Jean Stark, Wayne's devoted wife, always opened their home to students. She loved to talk to students and was a great supporter of Wayne and his vision for the MSC.[40]

From 1950 to 1970, the MSC worked to awaken a drab, structured military college and expose its students to a variety of amenities and programs that would impact their lives long after they had graduated and left the confines of College Station. Hector Gutierrez believed during this time that the only way Aggies, and particularly members of the Corps, could gain exposure to more "worldly types of subjects" such as the arts, travel, and cultural experiences was to get involved in the MSC. It is ironic that what was intended to be primarily an aesthetically pleasing building providing services and amenities not found within A&M at the time it was built turned out to have such a significant role in bringing cultural programs, diverse thought, and enriched leadership training to a conservative, highly structured campus largely identified by its regimented Corps of Cadets. As Jack M. Rains '60 so aptly describes, the MSC was a "cultural oasis in a khaki wasteland," and Wayne Stark believed in using the student center to provide students with a unique "classical education," one they were not getting in the traditional A&M classroom.[41] He exposed them to art but did not teach them art appreciation. He provided them with a glimpse of the workings and trappings of the business world but did not teach them the fundamentals of accounting. The MSC provided the classroom in which students could discover their thirst for art, music, politics, or travel and then acquire a taste for it. By incorporating cultural awareness, political consciousness, and leadership development into its programs, the student center became a portal to a much broader world than just the farms and small towns of Texas. These components were the tools needed to succeed in business, law, politics, and other fields. Stark understood that in order for A&M students to compete in the real world and live fulfilled lives, they had to gain exposure to things that most students at other universities could already access on their campuses or in their big-city hometowns. He wanted Aggies to have these same opportunities, and he knew the MSC would have to fill this role on a campus that was slowly working to transform in a fast-changing world.

THREE

A Cultural Oasis

1970–80

WITH THE ONSET OF THE 1970s, Texas A&M traveled a road of dramatic transformation. Women could now attend the school, the Corps of Cadets was noncompulsory for incoming freshmen, the formal name of the college had become Texas A&M University, and enrollment totaled fifteen thousand students. Over the next decade, enrollment continued to grow at an explosive rate and the increasing number of students, as well as their diversity, significantly impacted the MSC facilities and its programs. The student center remained the "living room of the campus," yet it became a bit more cramped with the burgeoning number of students. The MSC was still the place to meet friends, share a meal, watch TV, go bowling, check mail, or participate in the various student-led committees. This massive increase in the number of students directly correlated to a considerable rise in programming and usage of the MSC facilities. However, students were not the only ones who used the student center. The faculty and members of the Bryan–College Station community took advantage of all the amenities the MSC had to offer—the dining room, the banquet rooms, the conference rooms—as well as by participating in and attending MSC programs sponsored by committees such as Great Issues, Town Hall, Political Forum, and Arts. Indeed, the student center was many different things to people—a comfortable

The renovated MSC, featuring a porte cochere opposite Simpson Drill Field. The new Rudder Tower complex can be seen in the background. Courtesy Cushing Memorial Library and Archives

home away from home, a haven for rest and fun, a meeting place, a student development entity, and a cultural oasis. Yet all can agree the MSC or "C," as many students referred to it, remained the central gathering spot of A&M, constantly drawing in students, faculty, and visitors through its doors.[1]

Due to all this activity and foot traffic, it became very apparent that Texas A&M and the surrounding community had outgrown the MSC's facilities. The building desperately needed renovation and expansion to meet the needs of a growing university community. In fact, some might say the university was already on its way to outgrowing the MSC just a few years after it opened. As early as 1956, then chancellor M. T. Harrington had formed a committee to study the possibility of building a continuing education center next to the MSC, mainly for conferences and meetings. Although plans fell through for such an addition, interest remained and a former student announced that he would contribute fifty thousand dollars toward creating a west wing of the student center. While serving as university vice president, James Earl Rudder worked with an architect to do a feasibility study of rebuilding Guion Hall and extending the eastern end of the MSC until the two buildings met. In January 1966, MSC Council president John Rodgers '66 appointed a twenty-two-member committee comprising students, faculty, and staff to study the expansion of the MSC. The committee studied the feasibility of creating a new wing containing additional meeting rooms, lecture rooms, guest rooms, and other recreational facilities. In addition, they studied continuing education needs. This committee fully recommended the expansion of the student center to cover a then projected enrollment for 1976 of more than thirteen thousand students.[2]

In 1968, the A&M Board of Directors enlisted two architectural firms to conduct preliminary studies for the expansion and renovation of the MSC: Dede Matthews and Associates of Bryan and Jarvis, Putty, and Jarvis of Dallas. These two firms not only offered suggestions and costs for the MSC renovation but also looked at constructing a neighboring conference and theatre facility. The design for the twelve-story conference and theatre arts complex included housing the Offices of Continuing Education, Student Placement, and Student Aid, as well as numerous conference and meeting rooms. In addition, the facility included a 2,500-seat auditorium, a 750-seat theatre, and a smaller theatre seating 250. The Board of Directors approved the project, and construction of the approximately $28 million project began in 1971. Named in memory of President Rudder, who died in 1970, the Rudder Tower and Theatre Arts Complex opened in 1973. The timing of the expansion also allowed the university to rededicate the MSC as a memorial to Aggie men and women who died in all wars—past and future—since many former students had died in battle during the Korean and Vietnam Wars. The Rudder facility, along with the MSC, now made up what became known as the University Center complex. With its construction, the vice president for business affairs gained control over the expanded revenue-generating components of the new complex, including the MSC bookstore, food service, and conference-related facilities, and oversaw the operation of the student center's physical structure. The promise of additional revenue resulting from numerous conferences and more visitors to campus led the administration to centralize and ultimately direct this revenue flow and facilities management. Previously, MSC director Wayne Stark, with the input of the MSC Council, had the primary responsibility of managing all MSC facilities and services. But now, much of the student center's operations and maintenance fell under the direction of an administrative University Center board.[3]

As for the MSC, the building program did not significantly alter the original structure, but renovations did greatly transform its interior. Some of the changes included doubling the dining and cafeteria facilities to reduce overcrowding during peak dining hours and creating more lounge and study space. The Student Programs Office also moved into larger office space on the second floor and became the physical location for all student organizations, represented by hundreds of cubicles. Part of the MSC promenade was changed into what is perhaps the student center's best known feature—the "Flag Room"—due to the multitude of Texas, United States, and Corps of Cadets flags hanging in this main lounge. The entire project was completed in various stages, so as a new section became available, it opened for use. Although students did have

input into the planning of the renovations, several things on the "wish list" did not appear, such as additional bowling lanes, darkroom facilities, and a coffee house (students eventually converted a storage room underneath an outside stairway into a snack bar known as Rumours).[4]

Newly renovated and expanded, the MSC garnered a lot of attention due to its luxurious interior design. The A&M Board of Directors awarded the furnishing contract to William Pahlmann, an interior designer based in New York City. His "eclectic look" attracted several directors, including H. C. Heldenfels, who had seen his work in a variety of public buildings and private homes throughout the United States and abroad. Pahlmann favored a southwestern motif for the MSC, using imported furnishings, many of which came with an enormous price tag. In total, the furnishings for the entire University Center project cost nearly $3.3 million. Many students were not too impressed with the MSC's décor, citing its "gaudiness" and its "showplace" feel, while lamenting the loss of its previous comfortable, cozy environment. Students generally commented that the furniture did not seem suited to a student center. Both the extravagant cost of the furnishings and the items themselves raised many eyebrows and brought a flurry of articles across Texas, with titles and headlines such as "Elegant Uproar at A&M," "The Biggest Aggie Joke of All," and "Aggieland's Move to Opulence a Bad Gig." Reporters for the *Battalion* also wrote many articles about the exorbitant costs of the decorative features, even publishing photos of the interior with price tags superimposed upon pieces of furniture and décor. Their report revealed a nineteenth-century English oak center table costing $1,500, two $1,500 wooden globes, etched glass paneling surrounding the cafeteria featuring native wildflowers at a cost of $19,000, and the notorious thirty-seven steerhide benches designed by Pahlmann himself. Although they cost a total of $17,316, Pahlmann explained his use of these unique benches by saying, "This is cow country, so I figured why not use cowhide covers."[5] Another feature many students disliked was the series of mounted animal heads in the Flag Room. They included an ibex, a black rhinoceros, a waterbuck, a cape buffalo, and several others. Not long after they first went up, they came back down after the students openly complained and ridiculed their presence. Although the MSC received a fair share of negative publicity due to its costly new interior, the adjacent A&M Board of Directors Annex received even harsher criticism for its opulence and interior decorating cost of $765,000.[6]

While the University Center complex now provided additional space for student programs, conferences, and meetings, the theatre component of the facility provided Wayne Stark with the means to achieve his goal of exposing students to the performing arts right on the A&M campus. He recognized the importance of Aggies experiencing this type of culture, always making a visit to the symphony or ballet a key element

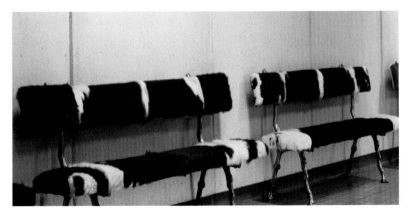

Some people believed the steerhide benches added to the MSC (c. 1975) fittingly showcased the deep rivalry between Aggies and the University of Texas Longhorns. Courtesy Cushing Memorial Library and Archives

of the annual MSC Spring Leadership Trip to Houston. Yet he longed to create a performing arts venue for A&M and the surrounding Bryan–College Station community. As preliminary plans for a theatre complex developed, Stark's longtime vision moved from being a dream into a reality. What better way to kick off a regular series of cultural presentations than to have it coincide with the opening of the new facility. As Stark later recalled, "The opening of the new building was the ideal—and almost the only—time to develop a concert series. It had to be together."[7] Up to that point, the performing arts partnership between MSC Town Hall and the Bryan–College Station Rotary Club, known as the Rotary Community Series, had brought artists to the area on a regular basis, having them perform at the Bryan Civic Auditorium. Stark envisioned a program much grander in scale and seized the opportunity presented with the opening of Rudder auditorium and its theatres. For years, as the university's size grew in terms of students and professors, more and more of these new members of the community were coming from metropolitan areas that had ballets, opera, and symphonies. When professors and their spouses relocated to College Station, they experienced a significant lack of cultural venues. One would have to drive to Houston, Dallas, or Austin to see a ballet performance, a well-known symphony, or a play. Margaret Rudder, President Rudder's wife, acknowledged "the fine arts group of the Texas A&M University Faculty Wives' Club sponsored bus trips to the larger cities in order to take advantage of cultural activities not available locally."[8]

Stark heard their complaints, recognized this large cultural deficit, and shared in their frustration. The construction of the Rudder theatre complex presented the perfect opportunity to move forward with his dream. With the support of A&M's president, Dr. Jack Williams, Stark pulled together several professors and their spouses, as well as some other community members and a few students. In the fall of 1972, he invited about twenty-five people to a meeting at a local restaurant where Stark presented his vision, an idea modeled after the structure of the Rio Grande Valley International Music Festival. Financial support for the music festival came from area residents, who formed a nonprofit organization. These residents solicited guarantors, who promised to pay one hundred dollars each in case receipts from the sale of season tickets, door sales, and donations did not cover expenses. Stark envisioned a similar structure working in the Brazos Valley with A&M and the Bryan–College Station community partnering together to create a performing arts entity. One of the participants in this initial meeting, Ann Wiatt, remembers how Stark even had a name picked out for the organization—the Memorial Student Center Opera and Performing Arts Society, to be known by the acronym OPAS.[9]

OPAS began as a nonprofit organization with about two hundred members, including community leaders, university professors, employees, students, and even some out-of-town individuals. In fact, Dr. David G. Woodcock, an architecture professor and longtime supporter of OPAS along with his wife Valerie, recalls each A&M department being asked to "identify 'missionaries' to recruit faculty to underwrite the OPAS season and purchase tickets."[10] Also, the OPAS Guild was formed in 1973 as an auxiliary community group designed to support OPAS through special events, educational programs, and fundraising. OPAS raised four thousand dollars in cash contributions and Stark secured two former students, H. B. "Pat" Zachry '22 and Tom O'Dwyer '47, as guarantors to help underwrite the inaugural OPAS season in 1973–74. On November 5, 1973, classical guitarist Christopher Parkening performed inside the new Rudder theatre, and a new era filled with world famous performing arts began on the A&M campus. The first season was a great success, featuring performances by pianist Van Cliburn in Rudder auditorium, Itzhak Perlman, the National Ballet of Washington, and the opera *The Marriage of Figaro*. Dr. Fran Kimbrough '69 remembers these early performances as "high-class" events for the entire Bryan–College Station community—"very formal and very sophisticated, with ladies wearing long evening gowns."[11]

From the very beginning, students participated in the OPAS organization. What would later become the OPAS Student Committee began as OPAS Hosts. The thirty-five-member student group served as official ushers and hostesses for all performances and events—taking tickets, distributing programs, operating information tables, and meeting performers upon their arrival in Bryan–College Station. Many recall those early days when students dressed in formal suits and evening gowns handed out programs. When OPAS expanded its offerings to bring musicals and Broadway-type shows in the mid-1980s, students took an even more active role in the decision making, planning, and management of the productions.

Staying true to the vision set forth by Stark, the MSC continued to be the major purveyor of various types of cultural programs, not only for the students but for the larger Bryan–College Station community as well. Students working on the MSC Arts Committee stayed busy producing enlightening programs focusing on art, literature, and live cultural performances, not an easy task when A&M did not even have a fine arts program or any related course offerings. Whether through films, dance troupes, lectures, production of A&M's literary magazine, or art exhibits showcasing local artists as well as the works of the masters from private collections, these students worked to provide Aggies with the opportunity to gain a fuller appreciation for these forms of artistic expression. Sometimes this committee brought controversial exhibits or films as part of its programming. One such case was in 1973, when the committee agreed to show *The Pink Flamingos,* a raucous, bawdy film many thought bordered on being pornographic.[12] Most of the time, the exposure to art was less contentious.

From the moment the MSC first opened, Stark had zealously "begged and borrowed" quality artwork for permanent display in the student center, and the MSC Arts Committee began to help him with this quest. Over the years, Stark had become the de facto curator for most gifts of art to A&M, mainly due to his interest and the lack thereof among the university administrators. Stark played a significant role in getting

OPAS STUDENT COMMITTEE

THE TEXAS A&M BOOKSTORE
in the Memorial Student Center
is proud to support OPAS
and the endeavors of its student members.

Students were active early on in the development of OPAS and worked diligently on the nights of performances, serving as ushers and hostesses. This particular photo shows the OPAS Student Committee for 1978–79. Courtesy MSC OPAS files

E. M. "Buck" Schiwetz '21 to become an artist-in-residence during the university's centennial celebration in 1976, for which he produced *Buck Schiwetz' Aggieland: A Portfolio of Eight Scenes from Texas A&M University.* Stark and the university procured various works of his collection, displaying them throughout the student center, particularly in the first floor lounge near the MSC main desk. Also to commemorate A&M's centennial, the university commissioned Dr. Rodney C. Hill, professor of architecture, to design and carve six beautiful wood panels depicting the hundred-year history of A&M, which now line the wall of the MSC's first floor east hallway. He and his wife, Sue Hill, spent years researching documents and photographs to help them create these amazingly detailed works. The walnut panels represent six important aspects of the university's heritage—A&M historical landmarks; the Corps of Cadets; sports and traditions; agriculture; veterinary medicine and science; and geology, engineering, and architecture. In the early 1970s, Stark began coordinating large exhibitions in the Rudder exhibit hall, beginning with a showing of Remingtons and Russells from the Sid Richardson Collection and the Amon Carter Museum. This series of prestigious exhibitions later evolved into the University Art Exhibits Program. Led by Stark, this program became the lead presenter of national, international, and museum-quality exhibits on campus. The MSC Arts Committee, which later became known as the MSC Visual Arts Committee, turned its focus to regional and local artists, still planning and managing all aspects of these exhibitions, while also assisting Stark with the University Art Exhibits Program.[13]

As the student body continued to diversify at A&M with the arrival of female students, more non-reg students, and minority students in earnest, the landscape of the campus was transformed with the construction of new buildings, civilian and female dormitories, renovations to old structures, and a flurry of additional extracurricular activities. By 1972, 10 percent of Texas A&M's total enrollment of 16,000 students were women. The Corps continued to dwindle in size relative to the growing civilian student population as it dropped below 2,000 members in 1974–75. In 1977, 111 African American students attended A&M. During the 1970s and into the 1980s, campus activities flourished to meet the needs of a rapidly changing student body, and the MSC still served as the center of student life. A variety of new MSC committees originated during this time period, offering programs of interest to these diverse audiences and the broader, growing Bryan–College Station community. Many female students first got involved at the MSC through the Host and Fashion Committee. This committee

came together with the purpose of presenting fashion shows and serving as hostesses for visiting dignitaries on campus. A group within this committee, called the Mam'selles, served as hostesses for OPAS and participated as models in the fashion shows. Dr. Fran Kimbrough '69 fondly recalls her experience as a Mam'selle, modeling in a Neiman Marcus style show held in the MSC's ballroom. Later, this committee became known as MSC Hospitality and broadened its scope to include service projects in local schools, such as reading programs and drug and alcohol awareness. It also gained the distinct honor of being the "Official Host Committee of Texas A&M University." Although Stark designed this committee specifically to get female students involved in the MSC and encouraged them to become active in other committees such as Great Issues and SCONA, some committees remained "unofficially" closed to them. Kimbrough acknowledged that she would have liked to join MSC Town Hall, but that committee was "kind of a male bastion."[14] A watershed moment came for female students in 1975 when Naomi Jane Logan became the first female president of the MSC Council. In a letter written for inclusion in a *Texas Aggie* article about Stark, Logan credits him with helping her "understand that it is possible to be an effective leader and manager without sacrificing any femininity." Stark later helped her get into the MBA program at George Washington University and, not surprisingly, called upon her as a former student to help out with worthy MSC projects in need of funding.[15]

Six A&M centennial wood carvings, unveiled in 1976, depict the history, life, and tradition of the university. These three-by-eight-foot detailed carvings were created by Rodney Hill and Sue Hill and are located on the first floor east hallway adjoining the MSC Flag Room. A seventh carving was added in 1998, a gift from the Class of 1993. Every tour of the MSC includes a stop in front of these remarkable panels. Courtesy Robert Bacon

Students working the Host and Fashion Committee booth at MSC Open House, c. 1975. Many female students first got involved in the MSC organization through this committee. Courtesy Memorial Student Center Director's Office

With more minority students enrolling at A&M during this time of rapid growth, the MSC took the lead role not only in providing a support network for these students but also creating opportunities to raise the awareness and appreciation of their diverse cultures. In 1974, the Committee for the Awareness of Mexican-American Culture (CAMAC) formed not only as a support group for these students but also to present programs to educate the campus as a whole about the Mexican American culture. This committee sponsored lectures, art exhibits, festivals, and programs featuring authentic performances such as mariachis and folk dances. Of course, the MSC Black Awareness Committee, which became a member of the MSC organization in 1970, continued to bring to the A&M campus exhibits, films, dances (including the Dance Theatre of Harlem in 1975), and speakers, such as Barbara Jordan, Alex Haley, and Julian Bond. A bit of controversy did flare up involving this committee when its leaders presented a list of demands at a press conference in 1973, calling for increased black student enrollment as well as black faculty members, the establishment of a Black Student Life Department, reorganization of the Black Awareness Committee into an independent organization separate from the MSC, and the designation of a "Black Room" in the student center. These demands were looked into by A&M president Jack Williams and the newly hired vice president for student services, John J. Koldus III, and tensions receded.[16]

As more and more students arrived at A&M, the MSC recognized the unlimited potential it had to offer through a variety of events and

programs on campus—to truly be the community center of the campus. The MSC Council stayed committed to this principle of the student union concept and initiated a host of programs and new initiatives to get students involved as soon as they stepped on campus, particularly in the MSC committees. Programs such as the MSC Open House, which actually began in the 1950s, became the premiere event to go to at the beginning of the fall semester, providing all new and returning students with the opportunity to walk among hundreds of booths set throughout the student center, where they could learn more about all the recognized campus organizations and the various MSC programming committees. The MSC All-Night Fair was a giant carnival spanning all three floors of the MSC, usually held on one spring semester night. Nearly a hundred student groups sponsored booths, games, and other entertainment for the entire evening, including a memorable "jail" set up in the ballroom by the Corps's Squadron 11. The MSC Recreation Committee organized programs centered around all types of games—billiards, ping-pong, bridge, board games, bowling, and later, fantasy role-playing games. Interested students gathered all over the MSC, at various times of the day and night, to participate in tournaments and special programs. In 1981, a subcommittee called GROMETS was formed within MSC Recreation to focus primarily on war games. In 1983, this group, along with the subcommittees concentrating on both role playing and board games, separated from the Recreation Committee and became an official committee called MSC NOVA.[17]

At the MSC All-Night Fair, Corps Squadron 11 traditionally sponsored the "jail" and could be seen roaming the MSC to "arrest" students and put them in jail. Courtesy Memorial Student Center Director's Office

Another organization designed for an imaginative form of student recreation actually began in 1969 with the creation of Cepheid Variable. This group of students shared a common interest in all things related to science fiction and fantasy and came together as a result of Science Fiction Week on campus. In 1970, Cepheid Variable became an MSC committee. Students worked together to produce specialized programming such as lectures, speakers, and movie presentations (including the annual showing of *The Rocky Horror Picture Show* at the Grove). Most of their efforts focused on the production of AggieCon, the oldest student-run science fiction and fantasy convention in the United States.

Given the dramatic influx of students coming to A&M during the 1970s and 1980s, the Bryan–College Station community could not keep up with the students' needs for various recreational outlets and entertainment venues. So the MSC tried to be "all things" to all the constituencies converging on campus and the surrounding area—a recreational center, a movie theater, a hobby center, and much more. As a past brochure stated, "It is whatever you want it to be . . . it is a building, . . . and it is programs. It's a one-stop, in-between class kind of world."[18] During this time, there was an MSC committee devoted to just about every pastime—MSC Camera, MSC Amateur Radio, which operated the station W5AC, MSC Crafts and Arts, and MSC Free University, which offered noncredit "fun" courses such as first aid, bartending, guitar, country-western dancing, and others. MSC Outdoor Recreation sponsored games and tournaments in table tennis, Frisbee, billiards, chess, football, and other activities, filling the role in what later became a part of the A&M club sports program. MSC Aggie Cinema continued to bring a wide variety of films to Aggies, filling a great void on the campus, as well as in the surrounding community. In 1980, there were just three commercial movie theaters in the Bryan–College Station area (one of which only opened on Friday nights and showed X-rated films). Aggie Cinema presented about fifty films per semester, offering a wide range of film programming on campus during the week and weekends, including popular, international, and classic movies. While this committee never shied away from exposing Aggie students to a diverse selection of films, most Aggies fondly recall Aggie Cinema as being responsible for showing popular movies at an affordable cost—a primary need among all college students.[19]

Likewise, MSC Town Hall continued to provide popular, contemporary entertainment to Aggies and community members on campus in G. Rollie White Coliseum or Rudder auditorium. This committee brought a variety of musical styles to the university community—pop, rock, country-

Elton John was just one of many top entertainers MSC Town Hall brought to Aggieland. Courtesy Cushing Memorial Library and Archives

western, jazz, and even Broadway plays. During this time, Town Hall had one of the largest budgets in the MSC organization and the students who participated in the committee were involved in all aspects of the shows—securing the contract, managing logistics of the show, hosting the performers, and ushering. Aggieland hosted performers such as the Eagles, Elton John, John Denver, Adam Ant, Hall and Oates, Larry Gatlin, Little River Band, Bob Hope, and the Charlie Daniels Band. Another committee, MSC Basement (later known as the Coffeehouse Committee), was formed to provide live entertainment in the intimate, relaxing atmosphere of Rumours, the informal snack bar in the MSC. Every Friday and Saturday evening, this committee presented talented local and university performers, offering a broad spectrum of entertainment—from country-western, blues, jazz, and rock music to comedy and poetry readings. Musical artist Lyle Lovett '79 was both a performer as well as a Basement Committee member, responsible for booking the local talent.[20]

Although the MSC busily added new committees to meet a wider range of needs and interests, many of the old committees continued to serve as the lead organizations in the MSC committee structure. SCONA increased its number of committee members as well as conference attendees. Continuing its tradition of tackling pivotal issues and questions reflecting emerging trends in American society and politics, the committee focused on a wide mix of topics ranging from American individualism to U.S. energy concerns, bringing in speakers such as H. Ross Perot, Senator John Tower, Barry Bruce-Briggs, and Dr. Milton Friedman. By the 1970s, SCONA had achieved national recognition as one of the largest student-planned and operated conferences of its kind. MSC Political Forum and MSC Great Issues also flourished, serving as the primary vehicles by which to bring distinguished speakers and political figures to the A&M campus. From 1970 to 1980, Political Forum sponsored lectures and debates among state and national political candidates, including then U.S. Representative Gerald Ford, presidential candidate Ronald Reagan, Senator Lloyd Bentsen, and other elected officials. Great Issues brought stimulating figures to campus such as respected world affairs correspondent Bernard Kalb; Louis Rukeyser, a renowned economics commentator; and Richard Levinson, TV/movie writer and producer of hit series including *Dr. Kildare, The Fugitive,* and *Columbo.* Through the efforts of these MSC committees, College Station was starting to become a legitimate stopping point for many national speakers, moderators, and lecturers.[21]

Due to the rapid growth of the student body and increased number of recognized student activities, the university administration responded quickly by creating a new administrative position and division to oversee all student functions on campus. In 1973, Dr. John J. Koldus became the first vice president for student services. He came from East Texas State University (now Texas A&M University–Commerce), having served as its dean of students and maintained a close affiliation with its student union. Koldus was very active in the National Association of Student Personnel Administrators (NASPA) as well as similar state organizations and was extremely knowledgeable about the student personnel profession and what it took to make things run successfully in regard to student services and activities. Koldus and Stark established a good working relationship, with Koldus regularly coming to Stark's office to visit with him and talk through upcoming programs and issues. Koldus recognized that Stark was known as "a fighter, fighting for what he thought was right—wanting the kids at A&M to have the finer things in life, for them to be cultured, and ultimately for them to have every opportunity in the world to be successful professionally and personally." Yet within the new vice president's office, Stark had solid support that was a bit foreign to him given his often impassioned encounters with

many past university presidents and administrators. As Koldus looks back, he recalls that Stark "argued with every president, in terms of what he thought was right and what programs we ought to have at A&M, . . . whereas now he had the support." Stark appreciated the fact that for the first time he had an administrator who actually understood what he was trying to do with student development and was genuinely interested in that area, rather than one who focused primarily on the Corps of Cadets.[22]

In 1974, given the enormous growth in student enrollment and their needs for additional activities, and also after consulting with all of his directors, Koldus reorganized the Division of Student Services and made significant changes he believed "tightened up the MSC to be the MSC," including creating the Department of Student Activities. Dr. Carolyn Adair, who had been a student programs advisor in the MSC, became the director of student activities, with the responsibility of assisting Student Government, Fish Camp, and various student clubs and organizations. Up until then, many of these organizations had been loosely under the MSC umbrella, some being advised by the MSC Student Programs Office staff and housed in the same location as the MSC committees. Adair came to A&M in 1962 when her husband Tom was working on his PhD, and she first worked for Stark when he established an assistantship in the MSC. Later on, she served as an advisor for several MSC committees, including the OPAS student ushers, Host and Fashion, Aggie Cinema, and the Travel Committee, with which she and Tom took A&M students on several ski trips to France. The creation of the Department of Student Activities and its separation from the MSC organizational chart was not without some growing pains, particularly for Stark, as this new department continued to be located in the student center. However, as Koldus recalls, "When we split off these other areas, what we agreed to was that university programming was Stark's responsibility through the MSC." Although Stark and the MSC committees remained the primary source of university programming, Student Activities and the MSC had to work hard at times to find a balance so as not to have student organizations producing similar programs or events. Occasionally, this arrangement created tension between the two entities, particularly as university policy changed. Prior to the mid-1980s, only MSC committees were allowed to do open-public, campus programming. However, coinciding with the explosion of special interest student organizations, that policy slowly changed over time to allow these groups to produce programs intended for wider audiences than just their memberships, and this opened up a new world of competition for the MSC.[23]

Wayne Stark adapted to this rapidly changing university atmosphere with his trademark professionalism. After all, he wanted Aggies to have a full college experience, receiving as many opportunities as possible for recreation, entertainment, and cultural enlightenment. Stark no longer had to focus on managing the MSC facilities and physical structure as he once did prior to the latest MSC renovation. While this change ultimately led to the loss of a centralized facilities management concept for the MSC, he did have more time to devote to his love of developing students. He believed the best place this leadership and community service training could take place was on the second floor of the MSC in the Student Programs Office. Stark structured each of the fifteen MSC committees in such a way that students had an enormous amount of responsibility and authority in producing their respective programs. Whether it be by procuring distinguished speakers to present at MSC Great Issues or MSC Political Forum, making logistical arrangements for MSC Town Hall or OPAS, raising funds for SCONA, or planning a $1 million budget, students received the unique opportunity to learn life lessons not taught in the traditional classroom. Lynn Gibson '77, MSC president 1977–78, recalls having signature authority for a million-dollar budget and remembers signing a contract to bring comedian Steve Martin to campus for one of his last stand-up tours. The MSC's reputation among other student unions across the country was that A&M's students got to actually put on programs, from beginning to end—a very unique experience not shared at other institutions. At the time, even the president of the University of Texas student union was amazed at the size of the

The MSC brought Steve Martin to the A&M campus, where the comedian entertained thousands of Aggies (c. 1977). Courtesy Cushing Memorial Library and Archives

MSC budget and the level of student management. Bill Davis '75, MSC president for 1974–75, remembers the University of Texas student being stunned over "the fact that students were running it [MSC], doing it, administering it—it just floored her."[24] It is truly astounding that MSC committee members had the responsibility and accountability for such a wide range of diverse programs, programs other institutions typically brought to their campuses through academic departments or alumni groups. In 1978, more than six hundred Aggie students were given the opportunity to develop their skills and abilities as leaders, managers, marketers, and even accountants in fifteen organizations they themselves created and sustained; they presented four hundred different programs to the A&M community. And like Gibson, all of these students did so strictly as volunteers.[25]

Of course, Stark assembled a talented group of staff advisors who supported the various MSC committees. It was their job to provide oversight and guidance to the student leadership while at the same time allowing the committee members to make mistakes and learn real world lessons. Many former MSCers fondly recall Colonel Harold W. "Hal" Gaines, who served as MSC associate director until his retirement in 1978. As Carolyn Adair remembers, Gaines was a "big old bear" kind of a man who was sweet yet could be very direct. As she puts it, "Wayne [Stark] was the vision-caster—the dreamer, and Colonel Gaines was the doer."[26] Upon Gaines's retirement, Stark then hired James R. "Jim" Reynolds to become the associate director. Reynolds came to A&M with a student center background acquired at Northeastern Oklahoma State University, Kansas State University, and the University of Kansas. With Stark now having no facilities-related responsibilities, he had the opportunity to focus all of his time and energy on students and former students. Paul Dresser '64 remembers that Stark's "standard pitch was to 'think big'— to stretch the imagination beyond one's hometown, immediate environment, relatively short-term A&M goals—and incorporate travel, unique experiences, business, culture, graduate schools, community service, and on and on into a 'can-do' plan."[27] Many former students heard time and time again his admonition, "Don't be a two-county Aggie," which meant experiencing life only in Brazos County and one's home county. In fact, Stark consistently prescribed graduate school and travel as the keys to becoming a well-rounded individual. By 1980, he had enabled approximately four hundred Aggies to travel abroad while serving as A&M's sponsor for the Experiment in International Living. His office overflowed with international objects as it became customary for each student to return with a memento of the trip for Stark. He also never let up on his zealous tactics of persuasion to convince Aggies to go to

A young Hal Gaines, sitting at his desk, gives students some advice about MSC affairs. "Colonel Gaines" was the MSC associate director until his retirement in 1978 and was widely admired by the students. Courtesy Memorial Student Center Director's Office

graduate school. He continued to be A&M's chief representative for the Harvard Business School—using his relationship with Larry Fouraker, by then dean of Harvard Business School, to full advantage, as well as working to guide hundreds of students in their application process to highly prestigious graduate programs and law schools such as those of Stanford, MIT, and Wharton.[28]

With that goal in mind, he skillfully used MSC committees such as MBA/Law to give students the maximum opportunity to understand the requirements for such programs as well as interact with representatives from various institutions and former A&M students who graduated from these schools. William H. "Bill" Flores '76 remembers attending MBA/Law Day when Dr. Fouraker would fly in and talk to Aggies about going to Harvard. He recalls how Stark zealously encouraged him to apply to the graduate program, saying, "I've got an application coming to you and I want you to fill it out, and I want you to bring it to me, and I want you to let me look at it."[29]

Back in 1970, Stark saw that many Aggies did not have the means to travel to some of the nation's most prestigious programs, so he organized what became an annual MSC program designed to give A&M students the chance to actually visit many of the northeastern Ivy League graduate schools—the MSC J. Wayne Stark Northeast Trip. Approximately twenty top upperclassmen and graduate students received the opportunity to visit the business and law schools at the University of Chicago, Northwestern, Harvard, New York University, Columbia University, and the University of Pennsylvania, as well as socialize with A&M former students at various receptions and events. These events brought together students and generations of "Starkies," giving him the opportunity to masterfully pair young Aggies with successful role models and mentors.

Perhaps Stark's most amazing quality continued to be this ability to match former students and others who had certain life experiences with young Aggie students who could learn from them. Kent Caperton '71 recalls how Stark helped him get a summer job at CBS News by calling upon a former student, Frank Manitzas '52, who was a CBS executive at the time. Caperton and three other Aggies worked the Republican and Democratic conventions in 1968, having the experience of a lifetime and instilling a confidence in Caperton that propelled him to serve as an MSC leader, A&M student body president, and later a Texas state senator from 1981 to 1991. Likewise, Don A. Webb '74 remembers how Stark arranged for him to spend one summer in New York City working with John S. Samuels III '54, who was a prosperous businessman as well as an influential figure on the New York performing arts scene. He served as chairman of the board for several arts entities, including the New York City Ballet and the New York City Opera. While there, Samuels introduced Webb to New York's finest museums, operas, symphonies, and ballets, even managing to visit an old J. P. Morgan estate that Samuels owned at the time. It was quite an experience for a young man from Arlington, Texas.[30]

U.S. Representative Chet Edwards '74 succinctly tells a similar story involving the great impact Stark had on so many Aggies. Edwards simply stated, "He changed my life and my career." By allowing Edwards to become a SCONA delegate his freshman year and subsequently urging him to try out for SCONA chair at the end of his sophomore year, Stark put a fortuitous twist into Edwards's life. The latter recalls Representative Olin "Tiger" Teague '32 calling his dorm room early one morning, trying to persuade him not to invite Ralph Nader to speak at the conference. Edwards stuck to his guns, Teague came to SCONA, heard Nader speak, and afterward sent a complimentary note to Edwards. On

A familiar sight—MSC director J. Wayne Stark sitting behind his desk and visiting with a student, most likely giving advice, promoting the benefits of attending graduate school, and planting dreams (c. late 1970s). Courtesy Memorial Student Center Director's Office

his graduation day two years later in G. Rollie White Coliseum, Teague offered Edwards a job as his first ever legislative director. When Teague retired from Congress in 1978, he encouraged Edwards to run for his seat. He lost that election but was elected to the Texas senate in 1982 and then to Congress in 1990. Edwards credits Stark with changing the course of his life and believes "the skills I learned in SCONA have been some of the most important leadership training I have ever received. One cannot put a value on the leadership development the MSC provided us." He also believes that Stark truly recognized the importance of making a positive difference in someone else's life and saw that as his calling at Texas A&M. He used whatever means necessary, including his loyal network of friends and former students, to help Aggies have unlimited opportunities.[31]

In fact, highly successful Aggies such as Teague, John Samuels '54, George Comnas '35, R. N. "Dick" Conolly '37, Jon Hagler '58, Bill Heye '60, James Howell '56, Weldon D. Kruger '53, John Lindsey '44, Jack Rains '60, and numerous others always remained on alert for Stark's phone calls during this time. They knew a call from Stark usually meant one of three things: (1) Stark, a masterful fundraiser, was calling to ask for funding for a particular MSC program, art project, or a student's travel expenses overseas; (2) he needed their help in finding a job or an internship for a student with high potential, or (3) Stark wanted them to host Aggie students for a visit. On many occasions, the call included requests for all three. As Paul Dresser remembers, Stark was constantly introducing him, in person or by telephone, to business leaders. He watched as Stark would "pick up the phone, call someone, and we'd have a conference call right there in his office."[32]

In any case, Stark leaned on his large network of distinguished protégés to help him pursue his vision for the MSC and in a broader sense, for all of Texas A&M. He wanted the MSC to be the university's beacon of culture and leadership. By being that beacon, the student center filled what many considered a large gap in A&M's educational offerings during the 1970s, particularly as the university scrambled to keep up with an ever-growing and changing student body. The MSC could fill the void until such a time when A&M's administrative and funding priorities broadened to include more diverse course offerings, particularly those pertaining to the cultural arts.[33]

Among Aggie students, Stark continued to be a highly respected, well-known figure on the A&M campus, but he was not known for just staying behind his desk and holding court. Rather, he remained on constant alert, trolling through the MSC cafeteria or walking its halls, looking for students who fit the "Stark treatment" profile—good student, rough around the edges, coming from a small town, perhaps a leader on campus, and almost always pursuing an engineering or science-related degree. In addition, he championed the liberal arts and doggedly persuaded engineering majors, accounting majors, and agricultural majors to take these extra courses. Ray Rothrock '77 credits Stark with helping him develop what became a deep appreciation for the fine arts by repeatedly encouraging him to take extra liberal arts courses every semester. Rothrock insists Stark "knew what buttons to push, so I took philosophy, sociology, and art history." Sometimes he could be insufferable, particularly if one was being "taken behind the woodshed" on the green couch. Chet Edwards '74 recalls sitting on the green couch as "more intimidating than any election day I've ever faced." Most would agree that although it might come across as him being critical, it was rather that "Mr. Stark was honest to a fault," as Robert W. Harvey '77 explains, "and he just delivered his comments straight." Yet most saw and appreciated his overwhelming love and devotion to students. As John Sharp '72 recalls, "He was one of the nicest guys that you've ever known . . . taking poor, bedraggled students, (who) for some reason he would see a glimmer of potential in. . . and just adopting them as his 'kids.'" Stark gathered students in groups, either at the MSC or his house, and talked about all the very successful Aggies he had known, telling one success story after another. Those moments and numerous others are when Stark worked his magic—planting the seeds in young Aggies' minds that these things were possible—and knowing one day he would be able to share their individual stories with the next generation.[34]

Whether he was approving MSC program requests, checking the SCONA speaker list, talking on the phone to a former student asking for some additional funds, or sitting behind his desk emphatically encouraging a student to think beyond his imagination, Stark unfailingly opened many doors for the students of A&M. But, in 1980, Stark brought his thirty-three years as MSC director to a close. He began to recognize his health limitations and retired, after which Jim Reynolds became the MSC director. Stark said his greatest pleasure had been "the contact with the students, those who just came by to talk and ask advice. It is very satisfying to watch a young student become involved with the university and grow as a person, getting an education that enhances what is in the classroom." However, Stark continued his remarkable service to Texas A&M after university president Jarvis Miller asked him to become special assistant to the president for cultural development, a position designed to promote the arts at the university. Given his immense network of former students and arts-oriented individuals, Stark formed and guided the 125-member President's Commission on the Visual Arts. This commission, a majority of which consisted of past MSC student leaders and current supporters, presented a comprehensive report to President Frank Vandiver and the chancellor in 1983, recommending the establishment of a major visual arts center on campus. At the time, the administration did not view this as a priority when placed alongside the longstanding needs for additional faculty, classrooms, laboratories, and equipment to meet the enormous growth A&M had experienced in the previous ten years. As a result, the MSC continued to serve as the primary purveyor of the visual arts on campus as well as all culturally related programs at A&M, a job not typically held solely by other student unions across the country.[35]

So when Stark retired in 1980, the MSC faced several daunting challenges. The first was to provide ever-changing, relevant services and programs to a diverse and booming population of students and a growing Bryan–College Station community—and to do so in an environment of newly formed campus organizations and community-wide entities, all competing for student volunteers, audiences, funding, and staff resources. The second was how to meet this challenge while staying true to the student governance component of the MSC—the idea that students had the unique opportunity to run MSC programs. An essential part of the MSC's leadership training included students sometimes making mistakes, producing less than successful programs, overspending their budgets, and then learning the necessary life lessons from these experiences. It was great training for students, but given the climate of the university at this time, with limited resources and a mushrooming enrollment, could the MSC still afford to operate in this manner? Would the MSC need to restructure itself just as the university found itself having to modernize its colleges and departments to meet the demands of a student body vastly different from the one that existed when the MSC first opened? The MSC and its new leadership entered the 1980s wondering what the future might hold for the beloved "living room of the campus."

FOUR

Presidents, Treasures, and the Bolshoi Ballet

1980–90

WHEN MSC DIRECTOR JIM REYNOLDS looked out his office window in the 1980s, he surveyed a vastly different A&M than what had existed a decade before. The campus stirred with an enrollment of nearly thirty-five thousand students, with less than 10 percent of the undergraduate student body participating in the Corps of Cadets. Female students made up at least one-third of the A&M student population, while more minority students, as well as international students, chose to make A&M their educational home. Now, about one-third of the university's student population came from the metropolitan and surrounding areas of Houston, Dallas, Fort Worth, and San Antonio. The days of an all-male military college comprising mainly Texas' rural sons seemed further in the past than a mere twenty years ago. The bold recommendations of the *Aspirations Study* of 1962 and the leadership of President Rudder had brought A&M to this point, saving the university as a major educational institution and propelling it into a higher level of academic standing. Indeed, A&M was becoming recognized not just for its unique military heritage, traditions, and the phenomenal Aggie spirit. In the 1980s and 1990s, the state and the nation were given frequent glimpses of the university highlighting all the school had to offer.

*James R. "Jim"
Reynolds became the
second director of the
MSC in 1980 and served
in the position for the
next twenty-five years.*
Courtesy Memorial
Student Center
Director's Office

The strategic plan adopted by A&M president Frank E. Vandiver in 1983, called *Target 2000,* contributed to great strides in enrollment, graduate and research programs, increased internationalization, and fundraising, all of which brought significant recognition to the university. Even A&M's dominance on the football field during this time did its part to expose national audiences to the A&M student body and its unique traditions, with thousands and thousands of former students, visitors, and members of the national press coming together in Aggieland during the fall. The place where these crowds gathered before and after a game was at the center of the A&M campus—the Memorial Student Center. Although challenges arose for the student center with the university's continued transformation, the MSC continued to be a leader in providing key services, amenities, quality programs, and distinctive student development opportunities to the A&M community in ways that broadened A&M's stature, brought respect to Aggies, and set a benchmark for other student unions across the country.[1]

When Reynolds took the helm of the MSC, he inherited an organization in need of restructuring so that it could effectively adapt to a rapidly changing A&M and continue to fulfill the mission of the student center. Reynolds, a native of Roxana, Illinois, earned a bachelor of science degree in zoology at Southern Illinois University and took an assistantship at the Museum of Natural History at the University of Kansas. However, he found his true niche within the walls of the KU Union, which stood directly across from his office. He took a job as an advisor there and proceeded to gain a variety of student union management and student development experiences there and at three other universities, including Kansas State and Northeastern Oklahoma State University. As MSC director, Reynolds wanted to focus on employing sound business management principles in the operation of the MSC, its student-led programs, and its student governance structure. Working with the MSC staff, program advisors, and students, he brought more emphasis to financial management and control processes, maximizing resources, adopting accountability measures, and engaging in more formalized leadership training. He stressed the importance of the MSC being able to produce quality programs, with high productivity and a good usage of resources. As Reynolds stated, "The better job we do in handling routine business practices, the more time the staff and I have to spend working with students . . . and be accountable to the administration and students of Texas A&M."[2]

The MSC Council underwent several organizational changes in an effort to fall more in line with managerial theories being practiced in business and industry, thereby better preparing students to function effectively in the corporate world. One of these organizational changes included adopting the concept of management by objectives (MBO), which provided the MSC committees with a sense of peer accountability. In 1980, Reynolds and MSC president Ernen Haby '81 brought in several former students, including Lowry Mays '57, to talk about this management theory, its use in the real world, and the benefits students in the MSC would gain by learning and implementing this practice. The

Cubicles for each of the MSC committees crowded the Student Programs Office (c. 1989). Courtesy Memorial Student Center Director's Office

MSC Directorate structure was dissolved, with the MSC Council now using vice president positions to oversee the activities of the committees. As Reynolds and former MSCers recall, there were definitely challenges and growing pains associated with these organizational changes, particularly struggles with the "council versus committees" mentality and budget review procedures. Yet the MSC leaders and committees took this energy and concentrated on making this more centralized business structure work in producing a host of programs with enormous benefit to the A&M campus and broader community.[3]

With the MSC producing additional diverse programs for ever-growing student and community audiences, few of these programs were inexpensive for the students to bring to campus. In fact, quite the opposite was true. It cost a lot of money to bring such a large number of educational, cultural, recreational, and entertainment programs to the campus. Reynolds recognized the importance of effectively budgeting for these costs, and he encouraged the MSC Council to institute a budget process requiring adequate projection, justification, and review. The MSC Council established the Budget Review Committee, which scrutinized the budget requests from twenty-seven programming committees. In 1984, the MSC operated on a $3.5 million budget, making it one of the largest college unions not only in terms of programs and student involvement but also in the size of its budget. Most of the funds came from a portion of student service fees, which in turn required the MSC to go before the Student Senate to "plead its case" for its annual budgetary needs. Generated revenue, such as revenue from the MSC Craft Center, Print 'n Copy, MSC OPAS, and the MSC box office, also contributed significantly to the budget. However, the remainder had to be raised by MSC committees, which actively solicited donated funds. This fundraising not only allowed the MSC to cover expenses but also, as MSC president Pat Wood '84 stated, "provides a learning experience for the students, which will help them their whole lives." Of course, fundraising was not new to those planning MSC programs, particularly not to SCONA, which was the first MSC committee to actively solicit donors back in 1955. The committee had to raise their entire budget because they received no student service fees. Yet with each passing year, whether it be other MSC committees or Wayne Stark asking a former student for the funds, the MSC as a whole engaged in more and more fundraising efforts, unmatched in scale by other student unions in the nation.[4]

In order to consolidate and expand these fundraising efforts, Stark, Reynolds, and "friends of the MSC" created the MSC Enrichment Fund at an organizational meeting in 1979. Consisting mainly of former MSCers, this group initially pledged five thousand dollars to help create an endowment for use in art, travel, lecture, scholarship, and leadership programs, thereby supporting these program areas for the future. To administer the Enrichment Fund, the group formed a board of directors consisting of twenty former students, six students, three faculty members, and several MSC staff members. The fund sought gifts in addition to those already given to the MSC through the Annual Fund of the Association of Former Students. The student center had been receiving a percentage of the Annual Fund, but with the enormous growth in programs and students, the MSC actively solicited donors and sought ways to effectively manage its fundraising efforts. A student volunteer position on the MSC Council, the vice president of development, supervised the fundraising activities of the various committees and worked with the MSC Enrichment Fund's board of directors to raise money for the endowment. In addition, this student maintained regular correspondence with potential donors, organized visits to campus, and planned annual fundraising receptions in Houston, Dallas, Austin, and San Antonio. One of the first students to hold this position, Becky Noah '85, praised the support of the Enrichment Fund board members, saying, "They take on the bigger needs—letting us use their offices, giving us names of possible donors, and setting up appointments for us." All of these efforts continued to assist the MSC with meeting its need to bring a large number and wide array of quality programs to the A&M campus. By the mid-1980s, approximately 1,600 students in the MSC produced more than 1,400 programs for more than 250,000 people each year.[5]

Heads of state, diplomats, politicians, distinguished lecturers, renowned scientists, cultural performers, and entertainers primarily came to A&M by way of the MSC. Indeed, it was during the 1980s that the MSC brought the greatest amount of national exposure and recognition to the university, not only through some of its established programs but also with the creation of new MSC committees and programs. In 1982, a group of MSC students believed A&M needed an annual lecture forum in which distinguished and well-known world figures could make appearances on campus. They transformed their initial concept into a reality by forming a charter and holding the first lecture program in 1983. This program, initially called the MSC Endowed Lecture Series, got off the ground with a lecture entitled "The Future of the Western Alliance," and it featured notable speakers such as former U.S. president Gerald Ford, former West German chancellor Helmut Schmidt, and former British prime minister Edward Heath. The lecture series was extremely well received by the university community and immediately established itself in terms of credibility and prestige. During the following year's program, two

*James E. Wiley Sr. '46
and his wife Virginia,
along with several stu-
dents, visit with Jimmy
Carter at a reception
during the MSC Wiley
Lecture Series in 1986.
The program in
1986 also featured
Dr. Stephen E. Ambrose,
former U.S. President
Gerald R. Ford,
and moderator
George F. Will.*
Courtesy MSC
Wiley Lecture Series
scrapbook

brothers in the audience, James E. Wiley Sr. and A. P. Wiley Jr., both from the class of 1946, were very impressed with the caliber of the program, which featured Henry Kissinger and Alexander Haig. James Wiley recalls being "quite impressed it was run completely by the students." His own son, James E. "Jim" Wiley Jr. '71, had been active in MSC programs as a student and as a former student. He served on the MSC Enrichment Fund board, working closely with Jim Reynolds. The younger Wiley had invited his father and uncle to attend the lecture, and later they contributed $500,000 to endow the lecture series program, which then became known as the Wiley Lecture Series. The unique component of the lecture series still exists—students produce the entire program from beginning to end. No other lecture series of its magnitude has maintained this type of student-driven management, planning, and implementation. Students receive the opportunity to learn life lessons and skills ordinarily acquired after students graduate. As Virginia Wiley, wife of James Wiley '46, emphasized, "These young people are given an opportunity to learn things that will serve them the rest of their lives, whether it's fundraising, or being at ease with important people." While choosing a topic concerning major world policy issues, the Wiley Lecture Series has featured some of the most celebrated politicians, dignitaries, and experts in the field. In the 1980s, lecture panelists included Presidents Gerald Ford and Jimmy Carter, Dr. Stephen Ambrose, Dr. Jeane Kirkpatrick, former British prime minister Lord Callaghan, Robert McNamara, William F. Buckley Jr., and *60 Minutes* correspondent Ed Bradley.[6]

National and international performing arts groups continued to find their niche on the A&M campus as MSC OPAS brought ballets, symphonies, plays, and orchestras to Rudder auditorium. Their various series exposed students and community members to performances by such groups as the Nikolais Dance Theatre, Rotterdam Philharmonic Orchestra, Great Gershwin Concert, Marcel Marceau, and the Tokyo String Quartet. In 1986, OPAS took over the booking of Broadway shows from MSC Town Hall, bringing the hit production *Cats* to sold-out audiences, as well as other shows, including *Singing in the Rain* and *Frankenstein*. Students also became more involved in the organization, with the student committee chair and other student officers continuing to serve on OPAS's board of directors. There, students could provide input regarding bookings, promotion, and other business items—working with leaders of the Bryan–College Station community. The responsibilities of the student committee members expanded beyond their early hosting duties to include publicity, audience polling, fundraising, and setting long-term goals.[7]

In November 1988, OPAS received the rare opportunity of bringing one of the most famous ballet dancers of all time to A&M. Anne T. Black, who became executive director of OPAS in 1987, succeeding James Randolph, remembers making a call to book the Houston Ballet for the traditional close-out show for the season. With the construction of the Wortham Center in Houston, the ballet no longer accepted two-night layouts but offered to do three nights of *Swan Lake*—for $150,000. Taken aback by their terms, Black desperately called the OPAS agent at Columbia Artists to try to find another ballet company of the same quality that could do two nights at a lower cost. As Black recalls, the agent called back saying, "What would you think about Rudolf Nureyev and the Paris Opera Ballet?" Black was ecstatic, even when the agent told her A&M would have to build Nureyev a special sprung wood floor. Black worked out an arrangement with Steve Hodge, the University Center facilities manager, to build the floor, and Rudolf Nureyev performed for sold-out crowds in Aggieland.[8]

MSC Town Hall also did its part to bring famous entertainers to Aggie students and the surrounding community. G. Rollie White Coliseum played host to such acts as the Commodores, Hall and Oates, Cheap Trick, Alabama, Air Supply, Jimmy Buffet, George Strait, Reba McIntire, and Randy Travis. Nearly one hundred student volunteers participated in

Town Hall, serving as ushers, helping set up the bands, and promoting the concerts through advertisements and posters throughout the campus and Bryan–College Station.[9]

During this time, other MSC committees such as SCONA, Great Issues, Political Forum, Cepheid Variable, and NOVA also continued to bring distinct recognition and large national audiences to the A&M campus. SCONA made a shift in its focus during the 1980s, concentrating primarily on U.S. foreign policy with conferences about Latin America, China, the Soviet Union, and the Middle East. Nearly three hundred student leaders from across the United States and other countries annually converged on the A&M campus to hear and discuss the views of ambassadors, foreign relations advisors, and renowned professors. MSC Great Issues presented programs relating to political, social, and economic topics, bringing nationally known speakers such as Michael Deaver, President Reagan's deputy White House chief of staff; Adrian Cronauer, the disc jockey portrayed in the film *Good Morning, Vietnam;* Dr. Ruth Westheimer; and Ralph Nader. More than one hundred student members of MSC Political Forum worked diligently to present programs and debates to educate Aggies about politics and current events. While striving to present students with a diverse array of viewpoints, Political Forum hosted a variety of speakers, including then presidential candidates George H. W. Bush, Michael Dukakis, and Libertarian candidate Ron Paul, as well as pro-family movement leader Phyllis Schlafly and Sarah Weddington, the attorney who successfully argued the pro-choice position before the Supreme Court in *Roe v. Wade.*[10] The committee made every effort to provide balanced political opinions, but MSC president Robert T. "Bobby" Bisor III '86, the first African American to serve as MSC president, recalled one instance in which the MSC became the center of a firestorm between Texas gubernatorial candidates and party politics. In 1986, Political Forum wanted to bring sitting Democratic governor Mark White and his Republican challenger, Bill Clements, to the A&M campus for a debate, yet they were unable to get a joint agreement from both campaigns. The committee attempted to conduct two separate programs featuring the governor and Clements as speakers. Unfortunately, Governor White did not want to take part in a separate program nor could committee members get anyone on the Democratic side to respond, so Political Forum continued to pursue Clements for a program entitled "Republican Perspective on the Future of Texas." George H. W. Bush, then the vice president, wanted to come and be a part of the program. Of course, as Bisor acknowledged, "You don't turn down an opportunity when the Vice President wants to come to campus." The media criticized the university as "cozying up" to the

*Jim Reynolds intro-
duces Vice President
George H. W. Bush to
a student during a
Political Forum pro-
gram in 1986.* Courtesy
Memorial Student
Center Director's
Office

Republicans, and it did not help matters when the Republican Aggies started mislabeling the event as a campaign rally. Bisor definitely got a crash course in public relations and how to respond to the media when he fielded numerous phone calls from Texas newspaper reporters.[11]

With a totally different focus, two MSC committees, Cepheid Variable and NOVA, also played a significant role in bringing big programs and distinct audiences to Aggieland. Cepheid Variable continued to host AggieCon, the oldest and what had become the largest student-run science fiction convention in the United States. Fantasy and science fiction dealers, artists, filmmakers, and speakers flocked to A&M once a year for this huge convention. Likewise, NOVA presented Warcon, an annual war games convention, which was the oldest known war gaming convention in Texas. Hundreds of fantasy enthusiasts and gamers from all over the United States attended these conventions, converging on the university campus and bringing a unique form of entertainment and recreation not typically associated with Texas A&M. The MSC recognized A&M's growing student population had diverse interests and, through such committees, worked hard to meet their needs and create a place for them to find common ground.[12]

As MSC director, Reynolds constantly emphasized that the MSC belonged to all A&M students, and he searched for ways to have each and every student involved in its activities. As he would say, "There's always room for more—more people, more programs, more involvement. We encourage any student, from freshman to upperclassman, to become involved in the MSC." Reynolds remained committed to the

AggieCon X

March 29 - April 1 1979   Texas A & M University

vision set forth by Wayne Stark, for students to have cultural opportunities and experiences outside the classroom walls. He worked hard to solidify the MSC programs organizationally and financially, seeing fundraising as an essential part of his job. Reynolds became quite the fundraiser. He picked up where Stark left off, nurturing the "Stark network," creating his own group of former students and supporters, and working to create endowments and other giving opportunities to fund MSC programs in perpetuity.[13]

One inspirational fundraising plan initiated by Reynolds and a large group of former students centered around honoring the man who had started it all at the MSC—J. Wayne Stark. For two days in November 1985, hundreds of former students and friends gathered to pay tribute to Wayne Stark and the wonderful influence he continued to have on thousands of Aggie lives. The Stark tribute featured speakers such as John Samuels '54, E. Lee Walker '64, Jack Rains '60, Chet Edwards '74, and many more who regaled the audience with Wayne Stark stories and memories. They even hauled the "infamous green couch" up from the MSC basement for the occasion, making Stark sit on it while they reminisced about his persuasive talks. U.S. Representative Joe Barton '72 shocked the unflappable Stark by reading a letter written by President Ronald Reagan, which said, "For nearly 40 years—since 1947—you have worked tirelessly for that great institution's educational and cultural development. Because of your efforts, Aggies are among the best educated and professionally motivated graduates in the nation."[14] Stark was extremely moved as the evening concluded with the announcement of the creation of the J. Wayne Stark Endowment for MSC Enrichment. Members of the endowment's steering committee—James M. Howell '56, Cherie Leavitt Haby '80, and Jim Reynolds—sent hundreds of letters to those influenced by Stark (names taken from his voluminous files and Rolodexes), reminding them that "he teased us with unimaginable goals, cajoled us into giving them serious consideration, badgered us into their pursuit, supervised us through their completion . . . and left us to think we did it on our own." They asked the former students to contemplate how much to give by asking this question: "Have your achievements been greater, your accomplishments more noble, your life's work more

During the tribute to him in 1985, J. Wayne Stark endures some good-natured ribbing from "Starkies" as he sits on his old green couch, brought up from the MSC basement especially for the occasion. Courtesy Memorial Student Center Director's Office

directed for having known this man?" Recognizing the importance of fundraising to the MSC's future, the endowment committee sought to raise $250,000 to help the MSC enhance its programs in the six areas of special interest to Stark—the performing arts, the visual arts, major lecture programs, special leadership programs, career and graduate school counseling, and international travel.[15]

Stark remained an important fixture at the MSC while he continued to focus on duties related to his role with the President's Commission on the Visual Arts. He moved out of the MSC Student Programs Office but stayed on the MSC's second floor, where students still gravitated toward Stark. Many MSC staffers such as Anne Black remember when he would come to the MSC director's office and ask if anyone wanted to go get ice cream at the university's creamery. Another relatively new staffer, Jane Bailey, participated in these ice cream runs and visited with Stark frequently—learning about his vast former student network and the MSC's institutional history. Before coming to College Station and assuming the position of assistant to the MSC director in 1985, Jane and her husband, Keith Bailey, were in the hotel and restaurant business in New Orleans and were General Electric distributors. A native of Greenwood, Mississippi, Jane Bailey also worked previously as a John Robert Powers model. Her life experiences, affability, and people skills made Bailey a true asset to the MSC, especially in regard to fundraising, public relations, and customer service. Reynolds also had her serve as the advisor to the MSC Council development officers, with whom she worked to solicit donors and maintain communications with former students,

Jane Bailey, assistant to the MSC director, started with the MSC in 1985 and for more than twenty years has helped hundreds of A&M students navigate the MSC organization, the university, the Aggie network, and life. Photo c. 1989. Courtesy Memorial Student Center Director's Office

friends of the MSC, and other potential supporters. Bailey became the "go-to" person in planning and producing social functions, out-of-town receptions, and major events associated with the MSC director's office. Students were immediately drawn to her warmth, her "no-nonsense" style, and her wonderful ability to counsel students about life issues. Just as Ruth Hewitt had done in the late 1960s, Bailey became the "second mom" to numerous Aggie students and Reynolds's right hand. Marc Carroll '91, a former MSC vice president of finance, echoes the sentiments of many students when describing Bailey as the "backbone" of the MSC and the "first person I sought advice from regarding MSC issues as well as personal matters."[16] Reynolds acknowledges her vital role in the MSC, observing, "Students don't leave their personal lives at the door of the MSC. They need time, attention, and assistance. Jane has been the one who has really stepped forward and taken on that role."[17]

In December 1986, the MSC continued to build upon its fundraising successes by procuring one of its largest gifts from a donor—a gift that brought significant international education and travel opportunities to hundreds of Aggie students. As early as 1972, Mr. and Mrs. Leland T. Jordan '29 had expressed to A&M administrators and Wayne Stark their desire to expose A&M students to foreign cultures and travel opportunities. Unfortunately, Mr. Jordan died in 1976, but, working closely with Reynolds, his wife Jessie carried out their shared vision by giving a $1 million endowment in the name of her late husband, thus establishing the MSC L. T. Jordan Institute for International Awareness. The Jordans had spent nearly thirty years overseas, beginning when he worked for Gulf Oil Company in Venezuela. He later became the CEO of Kuwait Oil Company, a joint venture of British Petroleum and Gulf Oil. To foster a spirit of internationalism at Texas A&M, Jessie Jordan established the endowment to help produce programs on international topics for the student body and surrounding community, as well as fund internships and scholarships abroad. She also donated their personal collection of international art objects to display in the MSC. This collection included valuable jewelry, porcelain, brass and silverwork, paintings, rugs, and furniture from South America, Europe, Asia, and the Middle East. Most of the objects were gifts given to the Jordans by dignitaries such as Queen Elizabeth II and the British royal family, the Shah of Iran, the Kuwaiti royal family, and Indira Gandhi. Several of the objects had once belonged to Queen Victoria, including a garnet bracelet and glass salt cellars. True to the MSC's student development and leadership training principles, the MSC Jordan Institute created a committee of fifty students responsible for all aspects of planning, organizing, and implementing the activities of the institute.[18]

With enrollment at A&M growing rapidly in the 1980s, it was not too difficult to see how the services, programs, and amenities required to adequately meet the needs of A&M students had outgrown the MSC facilities. Even after renovations to the MSC in the early 1970s, most administrators immediately recognized this shortcoming and knew the facility would require another phase of construction and renovation. In October 1984, Dr. Ed Davis, vice president for fiscal affairs, called upon the University Center Advisory Committee to begin studying the long-range needs and priorities of the University Center complex. This committee, consisting of the MSC director, the University Center manager, MSC president, student body president, director of student activities, director of the Office of School Relations, and the head of the Department of Theatre Arts, began soliciting input from student groups and committees. In November 1986, the A&M Board of Regents approved $15,000 to prepare program and design documents, and by 1988, the board had approved the design concept, submitted by the Fisher and Spillman architectural firm in Dallas. The estimated cost of construction was between $17.5 million and $22 million. The design concept called for additions to the north side of the theatre complex, including a five-hundred-seat expansion of Rudder theatre and a high-tech meeting room. Proposed additions along the east side of the MSC included expanding the bookstore, the choral music facilities, and the bowling/games area and creating a new food court. In addition, the expansion called for building a large new art gallery as well as an enclosed bridge between the MSC and Rudder Tower to house meeting rooms, a smaller student-run art gallery, the Browsing Library, and Print 'n Copy. The plan also called for a new building to adjoin a proposed parking garage on the site of what once was visitor parking across from Rudder Tower. This building would house student activities' groups such as Student Government, Off-Campus Aggies, and other organizations. Due to the flurry of student organizations being created with the increasing enrollment, the Student Activities Office, originally located in the MSC, had moved to the Pavilion in 1983 when it needed more space. The proposed building would house these student groups as well as the Placement Office, the Athletic Department, and the 12th Man Foundation.[19]

Before construction began in earnest in February 1990, some controversy did flare up about the project. One issue in particular concerned the preservation of twenty-nine mature oak trees that either had to be destroyed or replanted if the university undertook the project. One of the trees, the majestic Rudder Oak, was about 165 years old and thirty-three inches in diameter. Several faculty members in the Horticulture Department, including Dr. Benton Storey and Dr. Robert Rucker, as well as many students, openly opposed the expansion plan, citing its destruction of the oak trees. Many articles appeared daily in the *Battalion* calling for students, faculty, and staff to sign a petition against their removal. Although the plan moved forward as scheduled, university officials did attempt to transplant some of the oaks. Sadly, most of the trees were eventually replaced or destroyed, including Rudder Oak, which did not survive its move. Dr. Storey lamented, "I hoped it wouldn't happen and that I would be wrong, but it was a foregone conclusion that the Rudder Oak would die."[20]

As the 1980s came to a close and the physical appearance of the entire University Center complex began to undergo major changes, two groundbreaking events of historical significance and national prestige took place within the MSC organization, both involving the arts (an uncharacteristic "Aggie" field of interest) and both helping to build A&M's reputation as a world-class university. In 1989, the MSC Forsyth Center Galleries opened its doors in the student center in the location where the Association of Former Students had resided until 1987, when it moved to the new Clayton Williams Alumni Center. In this newly renovated space in the MSC, the dreams of Wayne Stark, Jim Reynolds, Bill and Irma Runyon '35, many former students, and numerous regents became a reality in the form of one of the most extraordinary art collections ever given to A&M. In the early 1980s, Bill Runyon (his wife Irma was deceased) wanted to combine his love for the university and for art

Students gather around Joe Arredondo '73, curator of the Bill and Irma Runyon Art Collections, as he describes a glass piece at the MSC Forsyth Center Galleries grand opening in February 1989. Courtesy Memorial Student Center Director's Office

by offering their premier collections, valued at roughly $21 million ($33 million in 2007), to the MSC to be permanently placed in the "center" of student life at A&M. Runyon was adamant that the art be completely accessible to students. Douglas R. DeCluitt '57, who at the time was a regent and member of the President's Commission on the Visual Arts, recalls Runyon wanted to "broaden the experience of A&M students through the presence of this displayed art and not have it stuffed away in a closet somewhere."[21] Runyon pressured the university administration to commit space in the MSC. As Reynolds remembers, it was Runyon's desire that the art be displayed in "a comfortable and welcoming setting, so that students would naturally be drawn into a relationship with the art."[22] Rather than have the academic side of the university administer the collection, Runyon wanted it completely managed by the MSC, giving students, particularly those involved in the MSC Visual Arts Committee, the rare opportunity to develop hands-on leadership and managerial experience with such an important art collection. The Runyon collection contains one of the world's premier collections of English cameo glass, including some of the best works of George Woodall, the preeminent English designer and carver. More than eleven hundred American and English glass objects, including some by Tiffany and Steuben, are part of the collection, as are sixty-six nineteenth-century American paintings, including important works by Mary Cassatt, Frederic Remington, and Charles M. Russell. According to Reynolds, this contribution, combined with the other art in the MSC, gave the student center an art collection

rivaled at the time by only one other student union in the United States—
Indiana University in Bloomington.[23]

Another watershed moment occurred for the MSC when MSC OPAS
landed what many in the industry saw as the performing arts scheduling
coup of the decade. In November 1990, the Bolshoi Ballet Grigorovich
Company emerged from behind the Iron Curtain and made its western
world premiere in Aggieland. For twelve days, Russian dancers received a
huge Texas Aggie welcome as they presented nine sold-out performances
of *The Nutcracker* in Rudder auditorium, as well as performances featuring the second act of *Swan Lake* and an evening of short classical dances.
The *Nutcracker* performance marked the first time in a twenty-five-year
period that a Soviet ballet company had performed the Russian classic
on a U.S. stage. The agreement between OPAS and artistic director Yuri
Grigorovich drew national and international media attention, with many
left wondering why Texas A&M had been chosen as the location for the
company's western debut. Apparently after touring more than thirty
other U.S. performance stages, Grigorovich learned of the special floor
OPAS had installed for Rudolf Nureyev's performance and he preferred
it to all the others. When the sixty Bolshoi dancers arrived in Aggieland
for their two-week stay, the story made headlines in newspapers around
the country, with hundreds of fresh, new eyes observing A&M at its finest. Aggie students walked around campus sporting T-shirts emblazoned
with "Bolshoi & Bonfire: The Hottest Ballet in Texas!" After the Bolshoi
premiere, MSC OPAS gained a new level of respect, as did the entire
university. A&M was now firmly on the map not only for its leadership
in agriculture, engineering, and military heritage but also for a unique
program sponsored by MSC OPAS, not an academic performing arts
department. Once again, the MSC filled a void at A&M, its mission and
its efforts helping launch the university into the next decade.[24]

At the end of the 1980s, scaffolding and construction crews began to
surround the MSC, working to provide a much-needed renovation to
keep up with the phenomenal enrollment growth at A&M. Yet inside
the student center, the tradition of quality university programming
and student development set forth nearly forty years earlier continued uninterrupted, the spirit never constrained by any physical limitations. In fact, during this time period, MSC students and staff constantly
broadened the MSC mission even further to expose A&M students to
all the world had to offer, setting lofty goals for the kinds of programs
and prestigious speakers that once might have only appeared on a wish
list. Their efforts to "think big" paid off handsomely for A&M, bringing a significant amount of national and international recognition to the
university. A&M had definitely begun to receive more attention due to

In November 1990, the hottest ticket in town was to see the Bolshoi Ballet Grigorovich Company perform in Rudder auditorium. The ballet company performed The Nutcracker *and the second act of* Swan Lake *almost nightly over a two-week period.* Courtesy MSC OPAS files

its excellence in academics, research, and athletics. National television audiences became quite familiar with the Aggie football team as they won the SWC championship three years in a row (1985, 1986, 1987) and won the Cotton Bowl in 1985, defeating Heisman Trophy winner Bo Jackson's Auburn team, and again in 1987, defeating the Fighting Irish of Notre Dame led by Heisman winner Tim Brown. Yet through the MSC programs of OPAS, Wiley Lecture Series, SCONA, Town Hall, Jordan Institute, numerous other MSC committees, and the opening of the MSC Forsyth Center Galleries, A&M garnered much recognition as a steady parade of dignitaries, politicians, heads of state, international performers, scientists, and national celebrities interacted with Aggies on campus. The MSC's grand successes in bringing such quality programs, all while serving foremost as the community center of campus as well as a student leadership laboratory, just reinforced what many in the college union field already knew from Wayne Stark and Jim Reynolds—the MSC was unique and an extraordinary asset to A&M. The MSC became the model to emulate among its peers, ranking as the largest college union in the country in terms of student participation and the number of programs produced for the campus and surrounding community. The future looked bright for A&M, and its student center remained one of its richest treasures.

FIVE

The Challenges of Change

1990–PRESENT

The MSC is more than a building or a place . . . it is a core element of virtually every Aggie's experience of Texas A&M. It serves to welcome members of our campus community, to introduce them to the breadth of activities and experiences available across the campus, to bring them together for interaction, to provide educational opportunities for leadership development and public service, and to be a place they always know they can come home to.

DR. DEAN BRESCIANI, VICE PRESIDENT
OF THE DIVISION OF STUDENT AFFAIRS, 2006

IN 1991, when the university completed the new construction and renovations to the MSC, the rest of the University Center complex, and the new John J. Koldus Student Services Building, a student body topping forty-one thousand now walked the well-manicured pathways of the A&M campus—a campus constantly growing and being transformed to meet the needs of its students. The student body received extraordinary opportunities to become involved in many organizations, activities, and programs both on and off campus. Whereas once the Corps of Cadets, the MSC, Student Government, and a few other organizations served as the major purveyors of the "other education" at Texas

A&M, the 1990s brought a dramatic influx of opportunities for Aggies to become involved in just about anything, whether it be the growing number of fraternities and sororities, active residence hall associations, or special interest groups like the Aggie Men's Club, the Dance Arts Society, or the Aggie Surf Club. Students entering the university during this time were looking less and less like their counterparts of ten years earlier. More and more students were coming from metropolitan areas as opposed to rural backgrounds. Many arriving on campus had already traveled internationally, and they were more likely to have their own cars, televisions, stereos, VCRs, and credit cards than the incoming freshmen five years before them. Admission standards were upgraded to include more emphasis on Scholastic Assessment Test (SAT) scores and high school class standings, bringing a growing number of honor graduates and National Merit Scholarship finalists and semifinalists to A&M. In addition, A&M was now a sprawling campus, one of the largest in the country. The campus, covering more than fifty-two hundred acres, was now separated into two distinct sections by the railroad tracks running through it—the main campus and west campus. All of these elements were the hallmarks of most highly ranked state universities, and to many around Texas and on the national scene it appeared that A&M had "arrived." With these changes occurring, the many new and daunting challenges the MSC faced were unlike any it had faced in previous years. For the first time in its history, the MSC found itself having to compete more and more for students' time, programming audiences, and limited student service fee support, not to mention the fact that the facility itself was no longer at the physical center of a vast, spread-out campus. Jim Reynolds, the MSC student leaders, and the committees entered the last decade of the twentieth century confident the MSC was a core element of Aggie student life—the primary social center of the A&M campus as well as one of its leading student development experiences. Yet at the same time, they wondered how to preserve its long-standing influence and relevance to a rapidly changing university and the surrounding community.[1]

While A&M was transforming itself physically, demographically, and academically, Reynolds and the MSC Council recognized the need for flexibility and fluidity in marketing and responding to the needs of its "customers" (students, faculty, staff, and community). Naturally, the first place the council evaluated was the entire organizational structure of the MSC and its intrinsic by-product—leadership development. For most of its history, the MSC's highly effective mission of student-led programming and leadership training was conducted in a mock corporate structure. The MSC used the 1990s as a period to reassess its managerial strategies, with Reynolds and the MSC Council wanting to be certain students received the latest type of training sought by the business world. Therefore, the MSC adopted several new organizational structures throughout this period, including the total quality management (TQM) approaches popular in the corporate world in the early 1990s and the concepts of servant leadership and other principles highlighted in Stephen Covey's book, *The Seven Habits of Highly Effective People* (1990). By the late 1990s, the MSC Council had adopted a matrix-style organizational structure after having engaged in an eighteen-month self-evaluation process. This process revealed that the organization had grown operationally cumbersome, with the MSC Council making almost all of the decisions and the programming committees having little or no vote. The new organizational structure added programming councils comprising similarly focused MSC programming committees. The programming committee level is where much of the decision-making process shifted for the entire organization, because these units actually produced the MSC's products, or programs, and thus could more effectively respond to the market and changing environment of A&M.[2]

On January 18, 1993, the university and the MSC lost the man many believed had played a significant role in initiating some of the transformations taking place on the A&M campus. J. Wayne Stark died at the age of seventy-seven in Bryan after suffering from a long illness, and with his passing, A&M had to say goodbye to a man who had done more for students than perhaps any other faculty or staff member in A&M's history. Given his far-reaching network of former students and friends, as well as his lifelong passion for student development, there is no way to estimate just how many lives he touched except to say it had to be an extraordinary number. A&M president William Mobley, who considered Stark a valued counsel and friend, noted at the time, "He is not replaceable, and A&M was fortunate to have him for so long. His legacy will be long-lasting."[3] Numerous former students, MSC staff, and friends came back to the MSC for his memorial service, during which Tom Fitzhugh '71 eulogized Stark with these words: "Wayne Stark did not voluntarily choose a teaching career. Yet he became a distinguished professor of life . . . this community, this building, this university were transformed through the dogged determination and dreams of this man."[4]

As for Reynolds and the MSC committees, they continued to stay true to Stark's vision and bring successful and cutting-edge programs to the A&M campus. However, several major initiatives on campus caused the MSC to find alternative ways to remain one of the major sources of campus-wide programming. Whether by altering some of the committees and the programs they sponsored or by dissolving a few committees,

J. Wayne Stark died in 1993, and hundreds of students and former students attended his memorial service at the MSC—the place where he affected the lives and futures of Aggies for more than forty-six years. The J. Wayne Stark University Center Galleries, located in the MSC, were named to honor his vision for advancing the arts at Texas A&M. The galleries display works from the university's permanent collections as well as traveling exhibitions.

Courtesy Memorial Student Center Director's Office

the MSC found ways to adapt to the changing campus environment and still fulfill its mission. For instance, the MSC Wiley Lecture Series was the primary vehicle by which to bring famous speakers, heads of state, and dignitaries to A&M and the Bryan–College Station community. As Deryle Richmond, MSC advisor to Wiley, recalls, "For the longest [time], this was the only vehicle by which those distinguished speakers would come to A&M." During this period, notable guests included Margaret Thatcher, Colin Powell, Jeane Kirkpatrick, Dan Quayle, General H. Norman Schwarzkopf, news correspondent Sam Donaldson, Soviet diplomat Nikolay Shishlin, and Vitaly Shiykov of the Russian Federation for Common Defense, plus many other world-renowned personalities. When the George Bush Presidential Library Center opened in 1995, world leaders and state figures began to come to the university regularly for special programs and lectures. Around this time, speaker fees for people of such stature had also become astronomical, nearly doubling. Again in 2000, professional fees doubled, particularly among the cadre of speakers MSC Wiley wanted to target. Richmond describes the fees as "the amount it used to take us to put a panel of people on a stage, it now takes for just one person." These factors might have destroyed the Wiley program, but the students on the committee recognized the need to establish a strong working relationship with the Bush Library. In 2001, Wiley wanted to bring Mikhail

Gorbachev in for the annual program. The committee had been interested in him for years, but his speaking fee was more than $100,000. So the Wiley students went to the Bush Library Foundation, asking if President Bush could make a personal request to have him come and accept a smaller fee. President Bush asked Gorbachev, he took a lesser fee, and that year twenty-five hundred people filled Rudder auditorium to hear him speak. MSC Wiley became the official student liaison to the Bush Library Foundation, with a committee member serving as the Bush Library liaison. Student committee members usher at Bush Library events and, along with the Bush School of Government and Public Service, cosponsor numerous roundtable symposiums and smaller lectures for the campus community throughout the year. When planning for the annual lecture series, Wiley committee students have been given a great resource for assistance in contacting high-profile political speakers, diplomats, and foreign policy experts. More recent lecture panelists have included Madeleine Albright, Walter Cronkite, South African president F. W. de Klerk, UN weapons inspection chief Dr. Hans Blix, and numerous other distinguished speakers. Yet the hallmark of the Wiley Lecture Series remained the same for students—to provide distinguished and entirely student-run programs. Wiley members become decision

Students gather around former British prime minister Margaret Thatcher during the Wiley Lecture Series program in 1993. Courtesy MSC Wiley Lecture Series scrapbooks

MSC Town Hall brought country-western sensation Garth Brooks, always an Aggie crowd favorite, to A&M on several occasions. Photo from *Aggieland*, 1991

makers, fundraisers, strategic thinkers, event planners, diplomats, negotiators, and even quasi security guards throughout the planning and execution of Wiley's main program.[5]

Likewise, the creation of another campus entity, Reed Arena, caused the restructuring of MSC Town Hall. In 1998, this 12,500-seat arena opened not only as the home of Aggie basketball but also as the major concert venue for the Bryan–College Station community. Up to this point, G. Rollie White Coliseum had hosted the major concerts brought to campus by Town Hall, including Garth Brooks, George Strait, Restless Heart, and R.E.M. The high cost of renting Reed Arena meant that Town Hall could not afford the major concerts it had previously presented. It simply did not have the budget. Rudder auditorium provided one potential concert outlet, but its capacity of 2,500 presented a major roadblock to Town Hall because the total ticket sales for such limited seating would not pay the cost of the entertainers. Working within this new campus scenario, Town Hall faced the challenge of continuing to provide high-quality yet affordable entertainment to Aggies. Town Hall organized smaller concerts with local bands and provided students the opportunity to perform through the Lunchbox Music Series held near Rudder Fountain, the Coffeehouse program, and the annual MSC

Variety Show. The MSC Variety Show originally began in 1951 as the Intercollegiate Talent Show and featured acts from regional colleges and universities. Over time, this committee evolved into the MSC All University Variety Show, which featured solely the amateur talents of Aggie students and faculty—singers, dancers, musicians, comedians, and magicians. The MSC Variety Show Committee members planned, organized, and administered every detail of the show, from advertising to logistical operations, and the show is held during Parents' Weekend in the spring. The Variety Show became a subcommittee of Town Hall, and its members remain responsible for all aspects of the show.[6]

Now that Bryan–College Station had sixteen commercial movie theater screens and a large majority of students living off campus, MSC Aggie Cinema had to restructure its mission to meet these changing dynamics. The committee changed its name in 1993 to the MSC Film Society and began to focus on bringing film awareness to Texas A&M. A student on the committee, Paul Alvarado-Dykstra '93, came up with the idea of having a student-run film festival on the A&M campus. Penny Ditton, a former advisor for the MSC Film Society, wholeheartedly supported his vision and remembers sending him "to Cannes, Telluride, Chicago, New York—every festival he could possibly go to. He was a real go-getter." Alvarado-Dykstra envisioned producing a competitive, invitational festival highlighting independent, minority, and student filmmakers from around the world. After lots of research and preparation, as well as Alvarado-Dykstra never "taking no for an answer," the MSC Film Society hosted the first Texas Film Festival in 1993, bringing film director Spike Lee to A&M as the inaugural guest of honor. His visit to campus sparked one of the largest media events in the university's history, bringing 130 journalists and other media representatives to A&M. Within a few years, the Texas Film Festival took off, garnering national recognition as the largest student-run film festival in the country. About fifty student volunteers worked during the week-long festival, which consisted of five nights of feature films and shorts, along with filmmaking workshops held during the afternoons. Over the next twelve years, the festival brought not only famous directors such as Oliver Stone, John Sayles, Robert Rodriguez, John Landis, and many other top names in the business but also a tremendous amount of publicity and national awareness. Perhaps the lasting impact of the festival can best be seen in the creation of a film studies program within A&M's College of Liberal Arts in 2001. Students can now earn a minor in film studies, and Ditton still recalls how the head of the program told her, "If there had been no Texas Film Festival on A&M's campus, there would be no film studies program. He said that it was only because we started the festival, that he was able to sell that idea to the academic department." This story truly epitomizes the historical relationship between the MSC and the broader university in which MSC programs have filled a void found within A&M at various times in its past. In many instances, the MSC has proactively caused A&M administrators and academics to acknowledge the importance of having such programs and fields of study and to incorporate them into the university's course offerings.[7]

Fortunately for A&M and the MSC, administrators, faculty, and former students were beginning to wake up to this point and recognize that although the university had come a long way from its humble beginnings, there was still work to be done in becoming a world-class teaching and research institution. With a student enrollment of nearly forty-two thousand, Dr. Ray Bowen took charge of a booming university, becoming the twenty-first president in 1994. He led the way for a major initiative that was built upon A&M's past strategic plans and designed to advance the university. Bowen, along with 250 faculty, students, administrators, former students, and other friends of university developed this strategic plan, *Vision 2020,* to position Texas A&M as a consensus top-ten public university by the year 2020. Initiated in 1997, this plan called for the university to pursue major imperatives such as elevating the faculty, improving graduate and undergraduate programs, building up the arts and sciences, strengthening professional education, diversifying and globalizing the university community, and enriching the campus. Of particular interest to the MSC was what role it could continue to play in advancing these imperatives. Some of the targets specified in the strategic plan, such as promoting effective student leadership training, advancing the arts, and globalizing the A&M community, had historically been the goals of the MSC through OPAS, the Jordan Institute, SCONA, Visual Arts, CAMAC, BAC, and the Wiley Lecture Series. The Division of Student Services, renamed the Division of Student Affairs in 1994 and led by Dr. Malon Southerland (upon Dr. John Koldus's retirement in 1993), and then by Dr. Dean Bresciani, firmly committed itself to operating all of its entities within the *Vision 2020* framework. When Robert A. Gates became president of Texas A&M in 2002, he actively embraced the *Vision 2020* plan and let it set the course for the university.[8]

Reynolds and the MSC Council sought to enhance MSC programs in the context of *Vision 2020* by proactively reviewing ways to improve its student programming and development experience. One area to improve upon was to broaden the leadership development experience to include even more Aggie students as well as continue to attract, cultivate, and retain a sufficient number of high-caliber student leaders to fill MSC positions each year. Given the enormous increase in these students' time constraints due to work, involvement in a whole new host of student organizations, special interest groups, and the booming Greek system, which now included more than fifty fraternities and sororities, the MSC found itself competing to draw them into its organization. The success and effectiveness of the student center's programs relied heavily on high-quality students becoming involved and staying on to produce and manage SCONA, OPAS, the Wiley Lecture Series, and other events. During this period, the MSC concentrated heavily on leadership training, making leadership and personal development one of its four major focus areas. It worked with a goal of developing more than one thousand students annually, equipping them to become model student leaders. This process took place within the student/staff partnership, long considered to be one of the MSC's greatest strengths. Yet at the same time, this organizational partnership presented unique challenges since 90 percent of MSC students changed positions each year. Reynolds and advisors such as Luke J. Altendorf were well aware of how continuity in leadership within the organization as well as the "momentum and synergy created by those leaders could oftentimes be lost during an academic year as students rotated in and out."[9] Therefore, the MSC sought additional ways to attract the most qualified younger students, improve their leadership development, and work to retain them as leaders within the MSC Council and committee structure. Reynolds and the council created several new leadership committees and programs geared toward this goal.[10]

One group, MSC Aggie Leaders of Tomorrow (ALOT), focuses on providing leadership development for freshmen as well as serving as a source of camaraderie. This program, known as Freshman Leadership Dynamics in the late 1980s, changed its name to ALOT and became an active committee in 1990. Throughout the year, ALOT members plan and participate in service projects and leadership events designed to give them managerial and leadership skills while also allowing them to make vital connections with MSC leaders, other student leaders on campus, and university administrators. One of their primary events includes hosting the Student Leaders of Tomorrow (SLOT) Conference, which brings more than 250 high school students to the A&M campus in the spring. This conference gives high school students a chance to experience the college environment while learning about leadership, and it provides an opportunity for them to network with speakers and A&M student leaders. The goal of the conference is to inspire these students to bring their leadership abilities to Texas A&M and the MSC.[11]

Incoming freshmen who are National Merit scholars and National Merit finalists are also given a unique leadership development opportunity through a special MSC program in collaboration with the Texas A&M Honors Program and the Study Abroad Programs Office. This program, the Champe Fitzhugh Jr. International Honors Leadership Seminar, was created in 1992 by former MSC president Tom Fitzhugh '71, who named the seminar in honor of his father. Citing the creation of the seminar program as one of the "greatest things I've ever done," Fitzhugh marvels at the success of the program, which has been a "great recruiting tool for the Honors Program, for the MSC, and a wonderful example of 'seed-planting.'"[12] Approximately thirty students are selected by application to travel on this two-week program to Santa Chiara, the A&M Study Abroad Center in Castiglion Fiorentino, Italy. Professional staff from the MSC and the Honors Program along with current student leaders accompany the new freshmen. The focus of the program is to expand the students' leadership skills and prepare them for the increasing responsibilities inherent in college life. The staff and student leaders serve as guides and resources throughout the seminar, providing leadership sessions on topics such as public speaking, team building, and conflict resolution as well as practical advice on everything ranging from declaring a major to how to live with a roommate. While the students are learning invaluable insight about the undergraduate experience, they are also given the opportunity to take side-trips through the Tuscan region, as well as to Florence, Rome, and Venice, thus gaining exposure to art, architecture, and other facets of Italian culture. The results of this leadership seminar have been highly successful in terms of getting students with leadership potential to become actively involved as soon as they arrive on the A&M campus, particularly in the MSC organization. Many of those participating in the Fitzhugh seminar have gone on to become committee chairs, executive directors, and MSC Council presidents. According to former MSC president Andy Liddell '06, "Most of my close friendships, my involvement in the Memorial Student Center, my participation in enriching academic experiences, and five subsequent adventures abroad are all because of the people I met through the Champe Fitzhugh program."[13]

MSC Freshmen In Service and Hosting (FISH) is another organization formed in 2000 by a group of former MSC Hospitality members. This committee became dedicated to not only helping freshmen develop leadership skills but also instilling in them a long-term sense of voluntarism. MSC FISH enables freshmen to learn how to plan and implement university-wide programs, service projects, and events. Some of the activities MSC FISH coordinates include the "Aggies Are We"

program, which provides international students a free monthly shuttle
to and from local grocery stores. In addition, MSC FISH members volunteer as mentors for the Boys & Girls Club of Bryan and do a variety of
other service-related projects. Given that Wayne Stark and Jim Reynolds
repeatedly emphasized to students the importance of giving back to the
community, MSC FISH put that lesson into practice just as MSC Hospitality has been doing for years.[14]

Another committee, MSC Leadership, Enrichment, Action, and
Development (MSC LEAD), started off as a committee in which students learned how to plan and implement leadership conferences (e.g., a
women's leadership forum) and other programs that applied leadership
theory. In 2002, the committee was restructured and became a sophomore leadership organization focused heavily on conducting university
outreach and recruitment programs. One program, Aggies Reaching
Out (ARO), sends Texas A&M students on a seven-day trip through
several South Texas cities where they work with junior high students,

Members of Aggies Reaching Out (ARO), a program of MSC LEAD, in fall 2007. Here they are shown with South Texas junior high students, with whom they establish A&M relationships and work to stress the importance of getting a college edu-cation. Courtesy Memorial Student Center Director's Office

helping them to understand issues within their communities, develop leadership skills, establish relationships with A&M students, and encourage them to obtain a college education, hopefully at Texas A&M. Another successful program, Aggie Shadows, offers local and area high school student leaders the opportunity to come to the A&M campus and "shadow" MSC student leaders in the fall and spring. Like the ARO, this program is intended to inspire these high school students to attain a degree in higher education and to strengthen their leadership skills.[15]

Along with the increased emphasis on developing the leadership potential and skills of younger MSC student volunteers, the MSC also during this period of time worked to expose these students to the impor-tance of leadership styles and values. Just like other graduates enter-ing the corporate world, Aggie students encountered organizations or colleagues engaging in unethical business practices. When talking with former MSCers, Jim Reynolds was struck time and time again with thoughts of how to better prepare students to face these problems at their work or in their communities and to teach them how to handle these situations. An opportunity presented itself in the early 1990s dur-ing A&M's "Capturing the Spirit" fundraising campaign (which raised a total of $637 million against an original goal of $500 million), when Frank and Joanie Abbott, the 1987 Aggie Parents of the Year, decided they wanted to give back to the university that had provided so many extraordinary opportunities for members of their family. As the Abbotts recall, the closeness of their family and their adherence to core values

Participants in the Abbott Family Leadership Conference, in which students examine the relationship between leadership, values, and ethics, in February 2008. A Saturday morning community service work project is also incorporated into the conference schedule. Courtesy Memorial Student Center Director's Office

made an impression upon Reynolds and his wife Pam during the many occasions they interacted. Reynolds believed there was a way to incorporate this sense of core values into an MSC program. With the encouragement of Jim Reynolds and his wife, the Abbott family proposed the establishment of a unique leadership conference in which students could examine the relationship between leadership and values. The conference would help them develop leadership skills based on ethics, values, community service, and the importance of family. Jimmy Charney '96, who was MSC executive vice president for finance, recalls sitting in the middle of the Abbotts' living room floor in Longview with a couple of other students, as well as MSC advisor Paul Henry, brainstorming how to structure such a program and organize the first conference. They encouraged the Abbotts to select sophomores and juniors to participate in the program because the MSC already had "freshman and senior leadership opportunities, but nothing for students in the middle."[16] In November 1995, the first Abbott Family Leadership Conference was held in Dallas, and fifteen student delegates were introduced to people who live and operate with strong moral and ethical values and incorporate those values into their businesses. Over time, the endowed conference evolved into two separate four-day conferences in Austin and San Antonio, and the number of student delegates has grown to more than sixty. All of the Abbott family, including David Abbott (a graduate of Trinity University), Preston Abbott '84, and Frank G. Abbott Jr. '86 actively support and participate in the conference while the student leaders of the committee plan, implement, and manage the details of the conference. The Abbotts firmly believe that what goes on behind the scenes in putting on the conference is just as important in student development as what the students learn from conference speakers, guests, and roundtable discussions. Frank Abbott emphasizes that the students are the ones who "plan it, raise the funds, they do the programming, and we do almost none of that. We may have an idea here or there, but we do not impose any kind of structure upon them." Reynolds is not aware of any similar student-led conference among A&M's peer institutions or at other universities across the country.[17]

In 2002, Bruce N. Spencer Jr. '37 also wanted to provide support for a leadership training and development experience geared toward sophomores. A longtime generous supporter of students through his President's Endowed Scholarship and Sul Ross Scholarship, he wanted to "bless them and help Texas A&M students maximize their potential."[18] He established an endowment to fund the MSC Spencer Leadership Conference held annually in Dallas. This four-day conference provides thirty sophomore students with the opportunity to participate in discussions and interact with prominent civic and professional leaders in business, industry, education, and public service, including many successful former students. This conference covers various topics, including leadership techniques and values development, and focuses on how leaders can use their influence and character to give back to their communities. As one attendee remarked, "This conference has been more than an 'experience'; it has been a life-changing mile marker for my life."[19] Although the MSC offers leadership training through all aspects of its committees, out of its current seventeen committees eight have a specific leadership focus or are leadership conferences reaching from the freshman to graduating senior level. Through its efforts to reach high school students, MSC LEAD, MSC FISH, and MSC ALOT are taking leadership training a step further and working to develop leadership characteristics in prospective Aggies.[20]

The MSC focused particularly on issues of diversity and collaboration with other student organizations and academic departments in the development of programs. Historically, the MSC has always championed diversity on campus. Wayne Stark recognized when the winds of change were blowing across the national landscape and always sought to have the MSC be a catalyst for social change at A&M. It was within the MSC that the Black Awareness Committee (BAC) found a home in 1970, as well as the Committee for the Awareness of the Mexican-American Culture (CAMAC) in 1974. Within the first five years of women enrolling in A&M, the student center was the only entity offering women leadership

Bruce N. Spencer Jr. '37 endowed the MSC Spencer Leadership Conference, which is held annually in Dallas for sophomore students. He is shown here in fall 2007 with a few Spencer conference participants. Courtesy Memorial Student Center Director's Office

opportunities within MSC committees such as Host and Fashion, Great Issues, SCONA, and Political Forum. When Naomi Jane Logan became MSC president in 1975, she was the first female to lead a major A&M student organization. Over the entire history of the MSC, seven female students have served as president of the MSC Council, which is a remarkable fact given that only three women have been A&M student body president. So the MSC responded proactively to the diversity initiatives outlined in *Vision 2020* in various ways. First, the MSC Council created a new committee, MSC Asian Cultures Education. Students on this committee sponsored programs that brought Asian cultural awareness programs to A&M. The MSC Woodson Black Awareness Committee (renamed in honor of historian Carter G. Woodson, the "father of black history"), along with a new standing administrative committee, MSC Diversity, work to bring programs and events that promote diversity sensitivity and appreciation throughout the A&M campus. Several MSC committees, such as Aggies Reaching Out (ARO), a part of MSC LEAD, and MSC FISH focus on reaching out to minority communities throughout Texas in an attempt to teach underrepresented students the importance of leadership and voluntarism, as well as to inspire them to pursue higher education and become Aggies. The MSC is one of the university's biggest assets in working to achieve Texas A&M's diversity goals.[21]

The MSC also collaborates on major university projects such as the "Campus with a Dream" program—a week-long celebration designed to commemorate the birth and ideals of Dr. Martin Luther King Jr. while

MSC CAMAC members with Luis Valdez, the noted playwright, writer, and film director who is regarded as the father of Chicano theatre in the United States, October 2007. He is the founder of El Teatro Campesino and directed the Broadway play and movie Zoot Suit *(1979, 1981), as well as the movie* La Bamba *(1987).* Courtesy Memorial Student Center Director's Office

increasing cultural diversity awareness on campus. In planning this program, various MSC committees work with the Department of Multicultural Services, the College of Liberal Arts, the Southwestern Black Student Leadership Conference, and other organizations. Reynolds and the MSC Council, always looking for opportunities to bring larger audiences to and greater participation in the MSC, began to embrace the idea of collaboration. What they discovered was that many organizations wanted the MSC to collaborate on such efforts because MSC student leaders had the reputation for having the experience, ability, and resources to produce high-quality programs. MSC Town Hall works with Aggie Yell Leaders to sponsor the annual "First Yell" event, which kicks off the Aggie football season with a weekend of fun activities and a Friday night show. Originating in 1998, this show has featured comedians such as Bill Cosby, Martin Short, and Wayne Brady. Collaboration with academic departments, student organizations, and other university entities helps the student center share expenses and provides non-MSC students, faculty, and staff with an inside look at the MSC's programming experience and expertise.[22]

In terms of the *Vision 2020* campaign's focus on infusing the fine arts into the life of the university, the MSC continues to be the major purveyor of the visual and performing arts on the A&M campus. Three art galleries reside in the MSC, each with unique collections and exhibits.

Located at the front of the MSC, the Stark University Center Galleries display works from the university's permanent collections, as well as traveling exhibitions. The MSC Forsyth Center Galleries, located across from the MSC post office, is home to the Bill and Irma Runyon Art Collections featuring American artists and one of the world's most extraordinary collections of English cameo glass. The MSC Visual Arts Gallery is a student-run art gallery, managed and administered by the MSC Visual Arts Committee. This committee provides students with

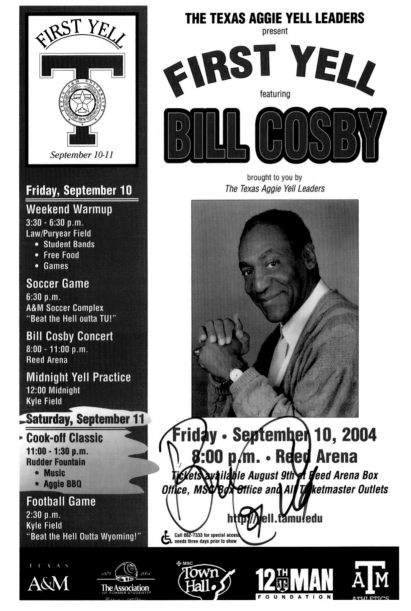

A poster for a "First Yell" event in 2004, which featured the popular comedian Bill Cosby. MSC Town Hall collaborates with the Aggie Yell Leaders every year in putting on this large event to kick off the Aggie football season. Courtesy Memorial Student Center Director's Office

Famed cellist Yo-Yo Ma gave a magical performance for MSC OPAS in December 2004 and is pictured on the right, along with A&M president Robert Gates and his wife Becky and pianist Emanuel Ax on the far left. Courtesy MSC OPAS files

hands-on experience in securing exhibitions, operating an art gallery, and producing educational programs complementing each exhibition. MSC Visual Arts even sponsors an artist residency each semester in which artists exhibited in the gallery present lectures to university classes and other campus groups. MSC OPAS continues to bring in world-class performers and shows such as Yo-Yo Ma, Van Cliburn, *Les Miserables, Rent,* and *Hairspray.* With each OPAS season, these performances provide Aggie students and community members with amazing cultural entertainment experiences, but the committee also actively sponsors arts education programs in the Bryan–College Station schools. In 2001, the Kennedy Center for the Performing Arts in Washington, D.C., recognized MSC OPAS's commitment to arts education by selecting OPAS and the Bryan and College Station school districts to become members of its Partners in Education program. Other MSC committees, such as MSC Town Hall, Woodson BAC, CAMAC, and MSC Literary Arts, regularly produce programs with artistic merit, including poetry readings, venues for original works of music, authors' presentations, and dramatic productions. The MSC's long-held commitment to arts awareness serves as a successful example for other A&M entities when working toward *Vision 2020* goals.[23]

As for international awareness, the MSC Jordan Institute is a true leader on campus, continuing to broaden its global scope by offering three different travel programs. The first is international professional internships in Australia, China, the Dominican Republic, England, France, Singapore, South Africa, and Spain. Students, selected through an application process, spend five to six weeks in a nonpaying internship while living with a host family. Another opportunity is the international service program, in which students spend ten weeks in rural areas of the Dominican Republic, Guatemala, Honduras, or Mexico and work in educational, agricultural, or health science related areas. The third program is the L. T. Jordan Fellows program, in which eligible A&M students receive grant monies from the institute to conduct independent study or research in any country around the world. Today, the MSC Jordan Institute is considered one of the flagship international study programs because of its innovative combination of campus programming and living abroad opportunities, constantly connecting Aggies to the world around them.[24]

Everything within the MSC was not always buoyant or without major challenges, particularly during this time of evaluating MSC committees and determining their relevance to the changing university around them. Some committees found it difficult to resonate with Aggie students, and their participation rates as well as the ability to attract audiences declined significantly. The MSC Pageant Committee, a group that originated under MSC Hospitality in 1980 as the Miss Texas A&M University Scholarship Pageant, significantly altered its focus during this time. The pageant began as an effort to select a representative who then competed in the Miss Texas pageant. However, in 1990, the purpose of the pageant changed, so rather than competing in the Miss Texas pageant, Miss Texas A&M was selected as an ambassador of the school, representing the university on campus and at special functions, including Aggie clubs across the state. In both formats, this committee served as a valuable training tool for many students as they learned how to produce a large-scale entertainment program. Students did everything from screening contestants, soliciting sponsors, advertising the event, creating the program book, selling tickets, and coordinating all the logistics of the event. As Ken Ballard '90, a former chair of MSC Pageant explains, "I learned valuable project management skills which still serve me today, both professionally and in my volunteer life. Being involved in the MSC inspired not only a drive to volunteer, but instilled a confidence to step forward and lead when necessary within my company and in volunteer organizations."[25] However, the MSC Pageant Committee was dissolved in 1995 due to a decline in interest among A&M students. Other MSC committees, such as Great Issues, Political Forum, Current Issues Awareness (a combination of Political Forum and Great Issues), and Insights, all tried to continue bringing programs focused on current affairs, politics, and world issues, yet competition for topics and speakers from the Bush School of Government and Public Service and from the Bush Presidential Library and Museum, as well as growing student organizations such as Young Conservatives of Texas and the Aggie Democrats edged them out. Even the MBA/LAW Committee found itself not needed as much on a Texas A&M campus where students from the Mays Business School now regularly received the opportunity to interface with business leaders, lawyers, and graduate school representatives. While it was disappointing to see the MSC lose some of its oldest committees, it showed just how far the university had come in being able to offer Aggies multiple opportunities to broaden their own horizons from a wider array of university-sponsored sources.[26]

Another challenge facing the MSC has been the increased competition for funding. Until the early 1980s, student service fees provided 65 percent of the MSC's financial resources. However, with more and more student organizations and outside programs competing to get larger percentages of the limited student service fee, the MSC recognized it could not rely on past levels of funding from this source. In the early 1980s, Reynolds and the MSC Council made a conscious decision to move the MSC from primary dependence on student service fees to primary dependence on generated revenue and proceeds from annual and long-term gifts. Generated revenues consisted of income from annual operations and sales of merchandise or tickets to events. Fundraising continued to be a primary objective of MSC committees, and the council structure actively supported this endeavor with student-led MSC Council development positions designed to coordinate the fundraising activities of the student center. The development area, led by the vice president for development and four directors, was charged with managing fundraising receptions and mailings, as well as working in conjunction with the A&M Development Foundation and the Association of Former Students to identify potential MSC donor prospects. In 1993, the MSC raised approximately $465,000 of its $3 million annual budget through contributions from individuals, corporations, and foundations. This fundraising component of the MSC, in which the primary fundraisers are student volunteers, is very unique when compared to the financial operations of other student centers. As Jane Bailey, assistant to the MSC director, insists, "We make a sincere effort to involve all students in fundraising at some level."

Similar student unions do not engage in the level of fundraising the MSC does, nor do they have student volunteers manage this type of activity or use the experience as part of their "real world" training. What is even more amazing is that these student volunteers tend to spend no more than one year in a particular leadership role.[27]

Yet rising costs of transportation, housing, food, airline tickets, and speaker fees continue to place an incredible burden on the MSC budget. In 2005, the MSC's budget totaled $6.2 million, with $2.4 million provided from student service fees. Approximately 42 percent of the budget came from generated funds (ticket sales, etc.) and 16 percent came from private gifts and endowments. Early on in his tenure as MSC director, Reynolds recognized the importance of creating endowments to ensure the long-term financial security of MSC programs, and he set this endeavor as one of his primary objectives. When he secured three of the MSC's largest endowments—the Bill and Irma Runyon Art Collections, the L. T. and Jessie Jordan Institute Endowment for International Awareness, and the Wiley Lecture Series Endowment, he laid a firm foundation for building the MSC's endowment base. Reynolds continued to research prospects, cultivate potential donors, and match their interests with existing MSC programs or with the creative development of new programs, such as with the Abbott and Spencer leadership conferences. The MSC estimates that for every student service fee dollar invested in the student center, the MSC returns $2.53 worth of programs and services to Aggie students and the surrounding community. While an increase in the student service fee would allow the MSC to produce additional programs and hire much-needed staff, the likelihood of it happening is very slim. In a referendum in 2003, A&M students voted down a student service fee increase. As a result, the MSC was forced to cut its budget and several committees were eliminated or decentralized, including Cepheid Variable, NOVA, Insights, Film Society, and Literary Arts. Components of MSC Film Society were given to other committees, with cinema being maintained by Aggie Nights and the Art House movie series being managed by the Visual Arts Committee. The MSC Council and Jim Reynolds did provide information on how they could reorganize their groups under the Department of Student Activities. Nonetheless, it was disappointing to cut these programs, and there was some resentment from those students directly affected. To maintain its level of programs and services, the MSC must continue to actively raise funds and build its twelve endowments. Reynolds, a consummate fundraiser, added significant gifts to the MSC's endowment program and encouraged MSC students to focus on this type of fundraising, as well as annual gifts. Former MSC president Jason Wilcox '91 knows firsthand how Reynolds worked diligently to raise funds and "keep the MSC in front of former MSCers—skillfully reminding them of their past while encouraging them to remember the MSC's future."[28] MSC students have a long list of former MSCers who preceded them, becoming successful in business, law, politics, and in their communities. The generous financial support of former students is extremely vital to the continued success and development of programming and leadership opportunities for all Aggie students.[29]

With so many changes taking place at the university, such as the large number of Aggies living off campus, the mushrooming of student organizations at the university, and the growth of the west campus across the railroad tracks, it might appear that the MSC has lost its status as the central gathering place for students, faculty, former students, and community members. One horrific tragedy revealed this to be far from true. In the early morning hours of November 18, 1999, the Aggie Bonfire stack collapsed with seventy student workers on the structure. Every year since 1909, before the annual gridiron contest with the University of Texas, Aggie students had pulled together to build and burn what became one of the world's largest bonfires. Although it began as a scrap heap and evolved into the more familiar and impressive stack of thousands of vertically arranged logs, the bonfire always symbolized the "burning desire to beat t.u.," as Aggies refer to their rival in Austin. It also became a massive symbol of the deep and unique camaraderie that is the Aggie spirit. Prior to 1955, Bonfire burned on what is now Simpson Drill Field in front of the Memorial Student Center. It was later moved to Duncan Field, behind the Corps of Cadets area. In 1992, Bonfire was moved again, to its final location on the polo fields.

On that fateful November morning, the logs shifted. The top three layers of the stack rolled over, trapping and killing twelve and injuring twenty-seven others. As word of the collapse spread throughout the campus, some panicked students ran to the scene, but hundreds began pouring into the MSC seeking information about those trapped and injured. Jane Bailey recalls Reynolds phoning her in the morning to tell her of the collapse and informing her "we're going to take over the Flag Room—there will be TV monitors set up there—and you need to handle food, drinks, and talk with these kids. There're going to be thousands of them coming in." As Bailey arrived, students were flooding into the Flag Room, crying and praying as they watched the monitors showing logs being pulled off students. After a while, lists came out with the names of the injured and deceased. Bailey remembers that "the students would surround me, wanting me to read the names of who was coming out of the stack and his or her condition."[30] Parents arrived and were led to Room 145 of the MSC, and each family was assigned an MSC or Student

The MSC Flag Room is every Aggie's "living room" on campus, drawing in students, former students, and visitors as well as being the central gathering place during times when the A&M community has needed to come together. Courtesy Memorial Student Center Director's Office

Activities advisor to remain there with them. Ron Fulton '76, manager for the MSC guest rooms, took some of the families who requested privacy to wait for news of their children in a guest room. He recalls that every time Bill Kibler, associate vice president for student affairs, approached the door of Room 145, "everybody in that room knew what he was there for."[31] Over the next three days, the MSC continued to be the place where dazed and grief-stricken students, families, faculty, staff, former students, and others would gather to comfort one another and find solace within the Aggie family. It was only natural that Aggies came to express their feelings in the "living room" of the campus.

Almost a year after the Bonfire tragedy, former students, Aggie students, faculty, staff, and friends of the Memorial Student Center joined together to commemorate a happier occasion and a major milestone in the student center's remarkable history—its fiftieth anniversary. Beginning in September 2000, the year-long celebration included multicultural entertainment during home football game weekends, a birthday party complete with cake in the main MSC hallway on the twenty-first of each month, and various programs sponsored by MSC committees to reflect on the five decades the MSC has served Texas A&M. In April 2001, the festivities concluded with a black-tie dinner and ball and a rededication ceremony on Muster, April 21, which recreated the first dedication held on the same date in 1951. MSC director Jim Reynolds emphasized the importance of celebrating the MSC's past because it "reminds those of us who are currently entrusted with the managing and programming of the MSC that we owe a debt of appreciation to those who have gone before us." Fifty years in the life of a building is really not a long time, but for a building that has served as the focal point in the lives of countless students and an entire university, it is a most significant milestone.[32]

From the outside looking in, the Memorial Student Center stands as a leader among student unions across the country because it has one of the biggest student programming and student development operations in higher education. The MSC also has perhaps the most valuable and most extensive art collections of any student center, particularly with the Runyon Art Collections, and it maintains with OPAS one of the last remaining campus/community performing arts series. It acquires more contributions annually than a majority of student unions. With a cash endowment base of $8 million and a total endowment of nearly $35 million, the MSC has more endowment money than other student unions. Through its efforts with the MSC Jordan Institute, the MSC does more international travel programming than any other student center and has an internationally recognized endowed lecture series with the Wiley Lecture Series. Throughout its rich history, MSC programs, administrators, and its student leaders have all contributed significantly to the mission and reputation of Texas A&M.[33]

First and foremost, the MSC will always stand as a memorial to all Aggies who have fallen in our nation's wars. As one walks through its halls, admiring the Corps of Cadets' flags in the Flag Room, taking the time to read about the Medal of Honor recipients, or looking at more than nine hundred names listed on the memorial plaque at the north entrance, there is a sense of patriotism and loyalty to Texas A&M that permeates the entire building. Like many Aggies, Lamar McNew '53, the third MSC president, contemplates the sacrifices made by those young

men every time he enters the building through that entrance. As he says, "My favorite thought of the MSC is the main entrance and what it stands for." It stands as a symbol of an Aggie's honor, love of country, and devotion to this school.[34]

Yet, just as important, the MSC serves as the community center of Texas A&M—the central gathering place for all members of the Aggie family to come together and feel at home on campus. The Flag Room, bookstore, dining areas, recreational rooms, and the overall environment that the MSC offers continues to attract students and visitors—it is essentially a "required" stop on any visit to Aggieland. Whether grabbing lunch, sitting in the Flag Room to study, meeting friends, or even heading upstairs to the Student Programs Office (SPO) to call potential speakers for MSC SCONA, this is the place where you find comfort, common ground, and a sense of community. As Jimmy Charney '96 puts it, "It is the come-together place—it's where you go on game day, it is where you start your tours, it's where you work in the SPO's tiny cubicles, and it's where you bring your parents, telling them about why they can't step on the grass and can't wear a cap inside."[35]

The MSC is the link that connects the university with the broader campus community, exposing both sides to the wide range of activities and experiences that take place within the building, are planned within

MSC director Jim Reynolds and former MSC Council members gather around the MSC-shaped cake at the student center's fiftieth anniversary kick-off party in the Flag Room in September 2000. Courtesy Memorial Student Center Director's Office

Colonel Vance Shaw (toward the left) is shown here in February 2008 with delegates who were members of his MSC SCONA 53 Roundtable and who won the award for best policy presentation. Shaw, a SCONA delegate himself back in 1962, is a dedicated friend and supporter of MSC SCONA and Texas A&M. Courtesy Memorial Student Center Director's Office

its walls, and then impact generation upon generation of Aggies. How that happens is the result of its role as an incubator of programs and leaders. The MSC is led by student committees, working together to develop campuswide programs to entertain, to educate, and to inspire audiences to go beyond the classroom experience and attain a much broader view of society and the world. From the time of its inception in 1950 and to today, the MSC enriches Aggies and Texas A&M and challenges the university to look to the future and meet the demands of an ever-changing university. While it appears that A&M has now "caught on" and is finally embracing many of the imperatives and core values historically espoused by the MSC, such as the importance of effective student leadership, international awareness, and exposure to the visual and performing arts, as well as the importance of diversity in thought and community, there were many times in the university's history when J. Wayne Stark and Jim Reynolds proactively used MSC committees such as SCONA, Great Issues, Visual Arts, BAC, CAMAC, OPAS, Cepheid Variable, and a host of other programs to fill fundamental cultural, social, and academic voids found on the A&M campus. Joe Arredondo '73, the former curator of the Bill and Irma Runyon Art Collections and also Stark's longtime assistant when he was both MSC director and special assistant to the president for cultural development, thinks what motivated Stark was his belief that Aggies would be "left out" of a world that values art, theatre, literature, performing arts, and music. Without this exposure, Arredondo says, Stark feared Aggies "would be caught short when they went out into their future jobs and communities."[36] By bringing attention to these shortcomings and finding ways for the MSC to meet these deficits until a time when the university matured enough to deem them a priority, Stark and Reynolds played a significant role in bringing A&M into the twenty-first century. Without their efforts and the historical programs of the MSC, Texas A&M, as well as thousands of Aggies, would have missed out on the opportunity to expand their worldview—to see world-renowned symphonies, engage in political discussions with U.S. presidents and world leaders, go on trips abroad, or learn to appreciate art by viewing exhibits of Old Masters.

Stark and Reynolds, with their solid belief in exposing Aggies to a broader worldview through vast programming and leadership opportunities, faithfully served the MSC and the university for a combined fifty-eight years. In July 2005, the MSC story began a new chapter when Reynolds moved to the office of the vice president for student affairs to become a development officer for the MSC. A year later, he retired from Texas A&M. For more than twenty-five years, he gave countless hours and complete dedication to Aggie students. He and his wife Pam devoted their time, energy, and hearts to developing students and helping them to broaden their experiences. Their home, just like the Starks' house, always remained open to students. At his retirement reception, hundreds of students, former students, and friends gathered to honor the indelible mark he left on the MSC and the university. During his tenure as director, Reynolds helped raise in excess of $60 million for the MSC, overseeing major milestones such as the creation of the MSC Wiley Lecture Series, MSC Jordan Institute, and the acquisition of the Runyon Art Collections. Former MSC president Frank M. Muller III '88 echoes the sentiments of many when he says that Reynolds was the right leader at the right time in the MSC's history. As Muller emphasizes, Reynolds was the "quintessential enabler, never taking ownership away from the students but allowing us to come to the right decisions through his guidance and the processes he set up within the MSC's structure."[37] Perhaps most importantly, he solidly built upon the foundation laid by Wayne Stark and developed an organizational structure capable of supporting a very large, predominantly self-sufficient organization. "If there's one item I wish to be on my tombstone at A&M," states Reynolds, "it would be that Jim Reynolds had the vision and courage to force the MSC into an organizational structure which has preserved a high level of responsibility and authority for *thousands* of students rather than *dozens* of students."[38]

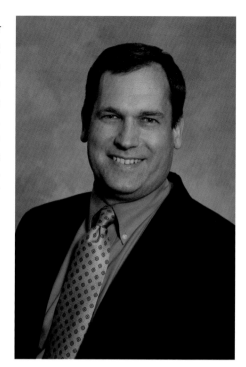

In 2006, Luke J. Altendorf, the associate director of the MSC, became the third MSC director and leads not only the student center but the entire University Center complex. Altendorf, who hails from Oklahoma State University, has worked at the MSC since 1987. He understands the MSC's unique history and its dual function of campus programming and student leadership training. Altendorf is an innovative, energetic leader who recognizes national trends in student development and leadership training and understands how student unions of today have to be willing to respond to the changing needs and demographics of today's modern student, especially in regard to programs, services, and amenities. He has a passion for working with students, "challenging them to grow as individuals, leaders, and involved citizens." He recognizes the importance of collaboration with other university organizations and believes he is uniquely qualified to direct the MSC, "having served twenty-four years as a student affairs professional and [been] privileged to have Jim Reynolds and J. Wayne Stark as mentors." There is no doubt he will greatly influence future generations of Aggies just as those two men did. The MSC's future is bright with Altendorf at the helm of one of A&M's most cherished symbols.[39]

On the second floor of the MSC, written above the entrance to the Student Programs Office, is the following statement: "Our goal is the development of persons as well as the intellects . . . a place where we may come to know and understand each other." The development and leadership opportunities afforded to Aggie students by the MSC, as well as through the tenacious efforts of Stark, Reynolds, and now Altendorf, are truly immeasurable. The results of this training, however, are very evident when looking at the positions of influence within A&M. One has to look no further than at the A&M Board of Regents, Association of Former Students Board of Directors, *Vision 2020* committee, *Target 2000* committee, the *Blue Ribbon* committee, the A&M capital campaign committees, the President's Commission on the Visual Arts, and numerous other advisory and development councils within the various colleges to see that many of their members are either former MSCers or earlier protégés of Wayne Stark. Former MSCers are influential players on Wall Street, in Fortune 500 businesses, law, politics, public service, and just as importantly, within their own communities. Promoting the MSC as a community center, leadership laboratory, and "cultural oasis," coupled with his zealous way of persuading Aggies to attend graduate schools such as Harvard Business School, Stark made sure Aggies had access to all the tools they needed to position themselves as leaders in their fields. As Bill Flores '76 emphasizes, "Look at the number of Aggies we have on Wall Street and the number of Aggies who go to Harvard, or Stanford, and have done well in business or participating in politics—a lot of that is directly attributable to the vision, influence, and cajoling of Wayne Stark."[40] Just one example of how his legacy lives on and resonates throughout the university is to look at "Aggies on Wall Street," a program sponsored through A&M's Mays Business School. This program is a two-week experience immersing students in New York's financial district. There, they meet and take classes taught by banking and investment firm executives, most of whom are A&M former students. Brent "B. R." Adams '89 acknowledges Wayne Stark's tenacious efforts to have Aggies experience New York and Wall Street, particularly through the annual Stark Northeast Trip in January, directly led to the development of this program. Only by utilizing the enormous resources of Stark's network of thousands of Aggies—a network and kinship that has survived him and continues to expand exponentially because of his rich legacy—could the business school produce this successful program.[41]

This immense network of former students remains fiercely devoted and indebted to Stark and his vision for Aggies. Most believe they would not be where they are today without his influence. Reynolds inherited this network, and over the next twenty-five years, he added scores of men and women to this special group by getting them involved in the MSC and working to make their experience a life-changing one. He challenged MSC leaders to reach beyond their limits, and that effort in

Participants in the MSC J. Wayne Stark Northeast Trip standing in front of the Rockefeller Memorial Chapel at the University of Chicago, c. 1999. This annual program, begun by Stark, is designed to give A&M students the chance to visit Ivy League and other prominent graduate schools, such as those at Northwestern, the University of Chicago, Harvard, New York University, Columbia University, and the University of Pennsylvania. Courtesy Memorial Student Center Director's Office

turn continued to make the MSC a standard of excellence for student centers around the nation and the world.

When one enters the MSC on a football game day, the energy is exhilarating as thousands of maroon-clad Aggie students, former students, and other fans fill the crowded Flag Room, bookstore, dining room, and hallways. There is no doubt the MSC is *the* place to be. Whether serving as a meeting place for friends, a gallery of diverse culture, a leadership laboratory, or as a refuge for studying, the MSC remains the living center of Aggieland. The building, the programs, and the leaders it creates are all a unique part of the Aggie experience and without it, A&M would simply not be the world-class university it is today. The Memorial Student Center continues to stand as a living memorial, a living room, and a living tradition of student programming, leadership development, and service—all of which are the very fabric of the Aggie spirit.

Epilogue

ON OCTOBER 10–11, 2007, nearly seven thousand students voted in a historic campuswide referendum, and 68 percent of them approved an increase in student service fees that will pay a large portion of an upcoming renovation to the Memorial Student Center. The student body of A&M, by then numbering almost forty-seven thousand Aggies (with projections forecasting fifty thousand students in the not too distant future), has once again outgrown the current MSC facilities—facilities that visually reveal the different styles and time periods of the original construction and previous renovations (1950, 1972, 1989). Many of its features are outdated and need better space utilization. According to MSC director Luke Altendorf, this renovation will "bring the building into the twenty-first century with state of the art facilities that will truly meet the expanding needs of A&M's growing enrollment, while continuing to serve as a memorial to those who have died for our freedom and serving as the living room and gateway to the campus." For more than a year, the MSC conducted a master plan study that brought together various user groups of the student center, including students, faculty, staff, administrators, and former students, to discuss with architects and facility planners their feelings and emotions tied to the MSC, their needs for space, their visions, and other issues. The referendum vote was the

first step in a four- to five-year renovation process that will ultimately result in a student center that respectfully honors fallen Aggies, serves the growing student population, and as Altendorf explains, "will create a bridge from the past to the future."[1]

Students, university staff, and architects will collaborate to create a design that combines service, style, and tradition (the Flag Room will remain untouched, as will the MSC grass). Concept plans and sketches, which are not final architectural plans or drawings, reveal what the MSC might look like and show changes such as a new café, additional dining options, extra room for student programs and activities, a Hall of Honor to show reverence for and respect to fallen Aggies, and more outside terraces, as well as a visually striking eastside entrance that will be more befitting of a building with such a rich tradition. Student space traditionally was one of the last priorities in the previous two renovations, so this project will significantly address that need. Out of 417,000 square feet of project space, only 71,000 square feet will be new construction. The remainder will come from renovating the inside. Current projections estimate project completion in 2013 and a total outlay of $100 million. The increase in student service fees will finance two-thirds of the cost, with the remainder coming from contributions and generated revenue.[2]

For the architects, MSC personnel, students, and other administrators who will oversee the project, the challenge is to stay true to the mission of the student union and all that entails, especially in today's consumer-driven, modernistic society, while preserving the most revered elements of A&M's beloved memorial. It appears that with the proposed Hall of Honor and the amount of attention and importance architects, planners, and students themselves placed on this aspect of the renovation, the end result should be an MSC whose role as a memorial is further enhanced and a student center that allows future generations of Aggies to experience this core element of the tradition and spirit of Aggieland.

Memorial Student Center Council Past Presidents

PRESIDENT	YEAR	COUNCIL
Joe R. Fuller	1950–1951	1st
Dan Davis	1951–1952	2nd
J. T. L. "Lamar" McNew	1952–1953	3rd
John S. Samuels III	1953–1954	4th
Charles Parker	1954–1955	5th
Herbert W. "Bud" Whitney	1955–1956	6th
Richard M. Wall	1956–1957	7th
Don D. McGinty	1957–1958	8th
Hugh Wharton Jr.	1958–1959	9th
Ronald E. Buford	1959–1960	10th
Weldon E. Lee	1960–1961	11th
Michael M. Schneider	1961–1962	12th
James E. Ray	1962–1963	13th
Howard M. Head	1963–1964	14th
Terrence Oddson	1964–1965	15th
John H. Rodgers	1965–1966	16th
Steven V. Gummer	1966–1967	17th
Scott H. Roberts	1967–1968	18th
Benjamin J. Sims	1968–1969	19th
Joe "Mac" Spears III	1969–1970	20th

PRESIDENT	YEAR	COUNCIL
Thomas C. Fitzhugh III	1970–1971	21st
John C. Dacus	1971–1972	22nd
C. Sam Walser	1972–1973	23rd
Don A. Webb	1973–1974	24th
William W. "Bill" Davis	1974–1975	25th
Naomi Jane Logan	1975–1976	26th
John Oeffinger	1976–1977	27th
Lynn Gibson	1977–1978	28th
Ray Daniels	1978–1979	29th
Brooks Herring	1979–1980	30th
Ernen Haby	1980–1981	31st
Douglas Decker	1981–1982	32nd
Todd Norwood	1982–1983	33rd
Greg Hawkins	1983–1984	34th
Pat Wood III	1984–1985	35th
Denis Davis	1985–1986	36th
Robert Bisor	1986–1987	37th
Linda Hartman	1987–1988	38th
Frank M. Muller III	1988–1989	39th
Jason Wilcox	1989–1990	40th
Matthew Wood	1990–1991	41st
Chris Britton	1991–1992	42nd
Rob Fowler	1992–1993	43rd
Heather Hartman	1993–1994	44th
Camm "Trey" Lary III	1994–1995	45th
Patrick Conway	1995–1996	46th
Christopher Williams	1996–1997	47th
Nellson Burns	1997–1998	48th
William Hurd	1998–1999	49th
William Anderson	1999–2000	50th
Nathan Cray	2000–2001	51st
Jennifer Brashares	2001–2002	52nd
Barry Hammond	2002–2003	53rd
Elizabeth Dacus	2003–2004	54th
Lindsey Wilson	2004–2005	55th
Andy Liddell	2005–2006	56th
Xuan Yong	2006–2007	57th
Jonathon Glueck	2007–2008	58th

Notes

INTRODUCTION

1. George Sessions Perry '40, *The Story of Texas A and M* (New York: McGraw-Hill, 1951), 31; Ernest Langford, *Here We'll Build the College* (College Station: Texas A&M University, 1963), 173; John A. Adams Jr. '73, *Keepers of the Spirit: The Corps of Cadets at Texas A&M University, 1876–2001* (College Station: Texas A&M University Press, 2001), 10–37; "Scores of Visitors Are Present for Opening of Student Center," *Bryan News,* September 24, 1950.

2. "MSC Offers Many Things to Many People," *Battalion,* August 27, 1984; Adams, *Keepers of the Spirit,* 238–39.

3. Frank M. Muller Jr. '65, interview by author, College Station, Tex., September 4, 2003; John S. Samuels III '54, interview by author, Galveston, Tex., October 18, 2003; E. Lee Walker '64, interview by author, Austin, Tex., March 17, 2004; Jack M. Rains '60, interview by author, Houston, Tex., February 7, 2005; Joe Arredondo '73, telephone interview by author, October 10, 2005; Drew McGehee '93, interview by author, College Station, Tex., August 7, 2004; *Comprehensive Program Review of the Memorial Student Center* (2002), 10, Memorial Student Center files, Division of Student Affairs, Texas A&M University (hereafter cited as MSC files).

4. Muller Jr. interview; Samuels interview; Sallie McGehee, interview by author, College Station, Tex., August 7, 2004.

5. Muller Jr. interview; Samuels interview; Drew McGehee interview; E. Lee Walker interview; Sallie McGehee interview; James M. Howell '56, telephone interview by author, April 23, 2004; Ray Rothrock '77, telephone interview by author, December 10, 2003; Robert L. "Bob" Walker '58, interview by author, College Station, Tex., February 18, 2004; "Stark Instrumental in Creating Student

Programs, Attracting World Leaders," *Battalion,* January 20, 1993; "A&M Programs' Developer Marks 40th Anniversary," *Bryan–College Station Eagle,* October 3, 1987. A common thread running through many interviews is that Stark was one of the first to establish such a thorough, expansive network of former students that he could call upon when in need of funding for a special program or to help place students in potential job opportunities. This legendary network was utilized extensively by Stark, and many recall the two massive Rolodexes that sat upon his desk containing the names of hundreds and hundreds of successful Aggies.

6. Tyree L. Bell '13, "Address at Memorial Student Center Dedication Ceremony, April 21, 1951," *Texas Aggie,* April 30, 1951, 1.

CHAPTER 1. A DREAM COMES TRUE

1. Adams, *Keepers of the Spirit,* 6, 11–12.

2. Ibid., 11–64; Perry, *The Story of Texas A and M,* 75–77.

3. Porter Butts, *The College Union Idea: As Reflected, Principally in the Writings and Addresses of Porter Butts* (Bloomington, Ind.: Association of College Unions–International, 1971), 9.

4. The Harvard Union was organized in a manner similar to that of the Oxford Union, consisting of several different buildings rather than a single facility.

5. Butts, *The College Union Idea,* 15–16.

6. Ibid.

7. "President Bizzell Plans Fitting Memorial for Our Fallen Heroes," *Alumni Quarterly,* November 1918, 4.

8. "New Memorial Student Center Begins Operations This Week," *Battalion,* September 7, 1950; "Union Building Again," *Battalion,* October 21, 1936; "The Y.M.C.A. (1914–): A Building Lost in Time" *Texas Aggie,* March 1997; "A Nice Room and Meals at a Moderate Cost: Aggieland Inn, 1925–1965," *Texas Aggie,* September 2003, 18; Langford, *Here We'll Build the College,* 104, 133–34; Perry, *The Story of Texas A and M,* 30.

9. Adams, *Keepers of the Spirit,* 132.

10. "We Need a Union Building," *Battalion,* March 11, 1936.

11. Ibid.; "Union Building Again," *Battalion,* March 31, 1936; Jeff L. Horn '37, "A Modern Miracle," letter to his fellow cadets, May 1937, "Buildings—Memorial Student Center," Special Subjects Folders, Cushing Memorial Library and Archives, Texas A&M University (hereafter cited as "Buildings—MSC" folder).

12. East Bell County A&M Mothers' Club Scrapbook, Cushing Memorial Library and Archives, Texas A&M University.

13. Adams, *Keepers of the Spirit,* 166; John J. Adams Jr., "Celebrating 125 Years, 1879–2004," *Directory of Former Students 2004,* 17, Association of Former Students, Texas A&M University, Clayton Williams Center, College Station, Tex. (hereafter cited as Association of Former Students).

14. William J. Lawson '24, "We Are Going Places," Muster address, April 21, 1943, Thomas O. Walton biographical files, Cushing Memorial Library and Archives, Texas A&M University; E. E. McQuillen, written presentation to joint session of Association of Former Students Board of Directors and Texas A&M Board of Directors, August 30–31, 1944, Minutes of Board of Directors, vol. 4, Association of Former Students; "Development Fund Objective Is Activities Center as Memorial," *Texas Aggie,* September 15, 1942, 1; *Texas Review,* March 20, 1946, Association of Former Students.

15. Porter Butts, "Report of Observations and Suggestions Resulting from Conferences at Texas A&M College, July 24–26, 1946," accompanied by cover letter dated August 5, 1946, 1–2, Porter Butts files, MSC files.

16. Bell, "Address at Memorial Student Center Dedication Ceremony," 1.

17. "Supplementary and Supporting Report—The Union Building Committee," President's Report to Board of Directors, June 25, 1947, 1–4, Agenda Book of A&M Board of Directors, Box 4, Cushing Memorial Library and Archives, Texas A&M University.

18. James B. "Dick" Hervey '42, interview by author, College Station, Tex., October 27, 2003.

19. "A Tribute to J. Wayne Stark" banquet program, November 9, 1985, MSC files.

20. "Memorial Student Center" information and room list, 1–3, MSC Folder (20 E), "Buildings—MSC" folder; "New Memorial Student Center Begins Operations This Week," *Battalion,* September 7, 1950; "Scores of Visitors Are Present for Opening of Student Center," *Bryan News,* September 24, 1950. According to Dick Hervey, several other architects, including Brooks Martin and Wally Scott, played a role in helping to develop the plans for the MSC. Hervey interview.

21. "Memorial Student Center" information and room list; "Ground Broken at Texas A&M for Memorial Student Center," *Fort Worth Star-Telegram,* September 22, 1948.

22. Hervey interview; "Student Center Entrance Now Has Memorial Plaque," *Battalion,* September 27, 1950; Bell, "Address at Memorial Student Center Dedication Ceremony," 2.

23. Dr. J. T. L. "Lamar" McNew '53, interview by author, Bryan, Tex., October 25, 2003.

24. "Scores of Visitors Are Present for Opening of Student Center," *Bryan News,* September 24, 1950.

25. Bell, "Address at Memorial Student Center Dedication Ceremony," 1.

26. "Center Is Dedicated in April 21 Ceremony," *Texas Aggie,* April 30, 1951.

CHAPTER 2. "HOW DID WE EVER GET ALONG WITHOUT IT?"

1. Bell, "Address at Memorial Student Center Dedication Ceremony," 1.

2. Stark tribute banquet program, November 9, 1985; "MSC Committees Outlined by Stark," *Battalion,* October 1950, in "Buildings—MSC" folder; Samuels interview.

3. Richard R. "Dick" Tumlinson '51, telephone interview by author, October 6, 2003.

4. John Whitmore III '51, interview by author, Houston, Tex., June 7, 2004.

5. "A&M Students, Community Use MSC for 'Living Room,'" *Bryan–College Station Eagle,* August 19, 1954; "'Living Room of the Campus': The 'Old' Memorial Student Center, 1950–1974," *Texas Aggie,* May 2001; "Gig 'em," *The Review* (Texas A&M University, College of Arts and Sciences), 6 (Fall 1964): 13–14; Robert L. "Bob" Walker '58 interview; "The MSC We Gave to A&M," *Texas Aggie,* February 1966, 4.

6. J. Wayne Stark, memo to E. L. Angell, August 9, 1948, 2, file 22, Box 5, and MSC Constitution, May 15, 1950, Box 5–23, both in President's Office Papers, Cushing Memorial Library and Archives, Texas A&M University (hereafter cited as President's Office Papers); "MSC Committees Outlined by Stark," *Battalion,* October 1950.

7. "MSC Special Edition," *Battalion,* Sept. 22, 1950.

8. Minutes of the MSC Council meeting, May 19, 1953, Official Minutes and Agendas, MSC Council, vol. 1, 1950–55, MSC files; "MSC Council Nods Rest of Budget, Names Committees," *Battalion,* May 20, 1953. In researching this topic for four years, I have yet to find any written documentation that definitively proves the memorializing of the grass originated when the building first opened.

9. Minutes of the MSC Council meeting, November 9, 1953, Official Minutes and Agendas, MSC Council, vol. 1, 1950–55, MSC files; President F. C. Bolton to Chancellor Gibb Gilchrist, March 18, 1950, Box 5–23, President's Office Papers.

10. "First Report of the Memorial Student Center," by J. Wayne Stark, n.d., Box 12–12, President's Office Papers.

11. Charles Parker '55, telephone interview by author, March 16, 2005; "'The Old D. J.': Parker Spins Discs, Perks Coffee for Morning Show," *Battalion,* January 8, 1953.

12. Samuels interview.

13. Herbert W. "Bud" Whitney '56 and John W. Jenkins '56, interview by author, College Station, Tex., October 25, 2003; "Café Rue Pinalle Will Open Tonight," *Battalion,* February 15, 1952; "Rue Pinalle Again Scheduled in MSC," *Battalion,* February 22, 1952.

14. "First Report of the Memorial Student Center," by Stark; Whitney and Jenkins interview; "MSC Art Exhibit Worth ½ Million," *Battalion,* February 26, 1953.

15. The Metzger Gun Collection is now known as the Metzger-Sanders Gun Collection and is at the Sam Houston Sanders Corps of Cadets Center.

16. President D. W. Williams to J. Wayne Stark, July 19, 1957; J. Wayne Stark to President D. W. Williams, July 25, 1957; President D. W. Williams to J. Wayne Stark, July 30, 1957, all in file 2, Box 34, President's Office Papers; "A&M Students, Community Use MSC for 'Living Room,'" *Bryan–College Station Eagle,* August 19, 1954; YMCA Freshman Handbook, 1958–1959, 49, and YMCA Freshman Handbook, 1960–61, 48, both in MSC files; "MSC Gives Students Place to Participate in Activities," *Battalion,* August 25, 1960.

17. Stark memo to Angell, August 9, 1948, 1.

18. Adams, *Keepers of the Spirit,* 166–67, 196.

19. Samuels interview.

20. Whitmore interview; Samuels interview.

21. "Class Distinction Blamed for Keeping 'Fish' Out of MSC," *Battalion,* September 24, 1953; Samuels interview; Whitmore interview; Stark memo to Angell, August 9, 1948, 1.

22. Whitney and Jenkins interview; "SCONA Draws 110 Delegates," *Battalion,* December 14, 1955.

23. Colonel Vance Shaw, telephone interview by author, October 19, 2006.

24. John H. Lindsey '44, interview by author, Houston, Tex., September 24, 2003.

25. Jenkins interview; Don R. Cloud '59, interview by author, College Station, Tex., October 8, 2003; Jon L. Hagler '58, interview by author, College Station, Tex., September 11, 2004; William B. "Bill" Heye Jr. '60, interview by author, College Station, Tex., October 1, 2004.

26. E. Lee Walker interview.

27. Hagler interview.

28. "The Memorial Student Center: A Look Inside" (group project paper

prepared by students of Gary Floden, PhD, Texas A&M University, Summer 1993), 31–33; Thomas C. Fitzhugh III '71, interview by author, Houston, Tex., October 22, 2003.

29. "Six More Regional Conferences Set," *Association of College Unions Bulletin* 17 (December 1949): 1, 3.

30. Adams, *Keepers of the Spirit,* 199–220; Henry C. Dethloff, *A Centennial History of Texas A&M University, 1876–1976* (College Station: Texas A&M University Press, 1975), 550–68; Dr. Haskell Monroe, interview by author, College Station, Tex., August 5, 2004; Bill Carter '69, interview by author, College Station, Tex., October 22, 2004.

31. Fitzhugh interview; "A&M Black Students Form Ad Hoc Affairs Committee," *Battalion,* February 21, 1969; Tom Fitzhugh, MSC President, memo to MSC Council members regarding Black Awareness Committee, August 18, 1970, Box 117–3, President's Office Papers; "Blacks Form Campus Group," *Battalion,* September 8, 1970.

32. "The Y.M.C.A. (1914–): A Building Lost in Time," *Texas Aggie,* March 1997; "A Nice Room and Meals at a Moderate Cost: Aggieland Inn, 1925–1965," *Texas Aggie,* September 2003, 18; Colonel Robert F. Gonzales '68, interview by author, College Station, Tex., September 11, 2004.

33. E. Lee Walker interview.

34. The "infamous green couch" was an old sofa that sat directly across from Stark's desk in his office. When one would sit on it, the person tended to sink deep into the cushions while Stark peered down from his desk. Almost every person interviewed for this book has a distinct memory of the green couch.

35. Patrick G. "Pat" Rehmet '68, telephone interview by author, August 24, 2004; Hector Gutierrez '69, interview by author, Austin, Tex., January 23, 2004.

36. Lindsey interview; "The MSC We Gave to A&M," *Texas Aggie,* February 1966, 14; Carter interview.

37. Heye interview.

38. Gonzales interview.

39. Muller Jr. interview.

40. Gonzales interview; Rehmet interview; Gutierrez interview; Jarrell H. Gibbs '60, interview by author, College Station, Tex., August 30, 2003; Sallie McGehee interview; Rains interview.

41. Rains interview.

CHAPTER 3. A CULTURAL OASIS

1. Memorial Student Center brochure, 1968–69; "Meeting the Challenge," MSC brochure, 1983, both in MSC files; Monroe interview; Sanders Letbetter, interview by author, College Station, Tex., September 18, 2004; Fred Dollar '44, interview by author, College Station, Tex., November 12, 2004.

2. "President Rudder's Charge to the MSC Addition Building Committee" and "President Rudder's Charge to the Auditorium Building Committee," January 11, 1966, Box 92–28, President's Office Papers; "Group to Study MSC Expansion," *Battalion,* January 11, 1966; "MSC Hot Spot of Controversy since 1950 Birth," *Battalion,* January 11, 1966.

3. "Board to Consider Plans for Big MSC Expansion," *Battalion,* January 9, 1968; "Students Not Consulted in Planning," *Battalion,* April 18, 1975; *Comprehensive Program Review of the Memorial Student Center* (2002), 7; "A&M Changing 'Hats

Off' Signs to Reflect Policy of Inclusion," *Bryan–College Station Eagle,* September 29, 1993.

4. Bill Davis '75, interview by author, College Station, Tex., November 13, 2004; "Programs Office Finds New Home," *Battalion,* April 4, 1973; "The Biggest Aggie Joke of All," *Texas Observer,* March 28, 1975; "Students Not Consulted in Planning," *Battalion,* April 18, 1975.

5. "A Palace for Aggie-dom?" *Battalion,* April 13, 1975; "The Biggest Aggie Joke of All."

6. Ibid.; "Elegant Uproar at A&M," *Houston Post,* May 1, 1975; "Aggieland's Move to Opulence a Bad Gig," *San Antonio Light,* May 7, 1975.

7. "OPAS—Stark Recalls Its 1972 Debut," *Bryan–College Station Eagle,* March 14, 1982; "The Story of the Opera and Performing Arts Society," premier season program, 1973–74, provided by Ann Wiatt; Ann Wiatt, interview by author, College Station, Tex., September 9, 2006.

8. David Woodcock and Valerie Woodcock, interview by author, College Station, Tex., September 2, 2006; "30 Years of OPAS," *Bryan–College Station Eagle,* September 2, 2002; "OPAS Past Performances, Memories," *Bryan–College Station Eagle,* August 23, 1992.

9. Anne T. Black, interview by author, College Station, Tex., April 20, 2005; David and Valerie Woodcock interview; Wiatt interview; "OPAS—Stark Recalls Its 1972 Debut," *Bryan–College Station Eagle,* March 14, 1982; "Story of the Opera and Performing Arts Society," premier season program.

10. David and Valerie Woodcock interview; Black interview.

11. Dr. Fran Kimbrough '69, interview by author, College Station, Tex., November 14, 2004; Wiatt interview; "Symphony Is Special Occasion for OPAS," *Bryan–College Station Eagle,* November 17, 1976.

12. Lynn Gibson '77, interview by author, Friendswood, Tex., July 31, 2004; Dr. John J. Koldus, interview by author, College Station, Tex., August 5, 2004.

13. James R. Reynolds, Presentation to the Executive Committee of the President's Commission on the Visual Arts, April 1, 1988, History of the Commission on Visual Arts file, MSC files; Stark tribute banquet program, November 9, 1985.

14. Kimbrough interview.

15. Naomi J. Logan to Jerry C. Cooper, editor of *Texas Aggie,* April 13, 1981, J. Wayne Stark biographical file (1971–84), Cushing Memorial Library and Archives, Texas A&M University.

16. Fitzhugh interview; "Blacks Announce List of Demands," *Bryan–College Station Eagle,* November 16, 1973.

17. "The Memorial Student Center: A Look Inside," 58–59; "Meeting the Challenge" MSC brochure, 1983; Pete Christian, "How NOVA Began," Association of Old Novads, http://ares.redsword.com/nova/origin.html (n.d.).

18. Memorial Student Center brochure, 1968–1969, 2.

19. Gibson interview; James R. Reynolds, interviews by author, College Station, Tex., October 28, 2005, and April 18, 2006; "25 Exceptional Years," *Texas Aggie,* March 1976, 11; "People, Places, and Programs—MSC Is Nerve Center of Campus," *Texas A&M Today,* 1983, 2, "MSC Programs–General" folder, Special Subjects Folders, Cushing Memorial Library & Archives, Texas A&M University.

20. "People, Places, and Programs," 2; *Aggieland,* 1980, 61–63, 1981, 54–58, and 1985, 58–61; "Some May Boast," *Texas Aggie,* November–December 2004, 29–30; "Meeting the Challenge" MSC brochure, 1983.

21. "25 Exceptional Years," *Texas Aggie,* 11; "People, Places, and Programs," 2.

22. Koldus interview.

23. Ibid.; "Koldus Revamps Student Services," *Battalion,* July 31, 1974; Dr. Carolyn Adair '69, telephone interview by author, October 25, 2007; *Comprehensive Program Review of the Memorial Student Center* (2002), 9, 44; Reynolds interviews.

24. Davis interview.

25. Gibson interview; "People, Places, and Programs"; *Comprehensive Program Review of the Memorial Student Center* (2002), 6, 17, 35–36.

26. Adair interview.

27. "He Strikes the Sparks in Aggies' Lives," *Texas Aggie,* May 1982, 25; Paul Dresser '64, telephone interview by author, September 6, 2006.

28. Weldon D. Kruger '53, interview by author, College Station, Tex., September 16, 2005; "He Strikes the Sparks," 25–27; "Pacesetter—A&M's Stark Makes Ideas Real," *Bryan–College Station Eagle,* March 27, 1983; Rothrock interview; Davis interview.

29. William H. "Bill" Flores '76, interview by author, Houston, Tex., November 10, 2003.

30. Kent Caperton '71, interview by author, Austin, Tex., January 22, 2004; Don A. Webb '71, interview by author, College Station, Tex., November 12, 2004; Samuels interview.

31. Chet Edwards '74, telephone interview by author, September 27, 2006.

32. Dresser interview.

33. Kruger interview; Lindsey interview, Rains interview, Samuels interview.

34. Rothrock interview; Edwards interview; John Sharp '72, telephone interview by author, September 8, 2004; Robert W. Harvey '77, interview by author, Houston, Tex., October 30, 2007.

35. "A&M Programs' Developer Marks 40th Anniversary," *Bryan–College Station Eagle,* October 3, 1987; Reynolds, Presentation to the Executive Committee of the President's Commission on the Visual Arts, April 1, 1988; Jim Reynolds to Getty Foundation, addendum I, July 7, 1986, History of the Commission on Visual Arts file, MSC files.

CHAPTER 4. PRESIDENTS, TREASURES, AND THE BOLSHOI BALLET

1. Reynolds interviews; Adams, *Keepers of the Spirit,* 264–80; Texas A&M University, *Vision 2020: Creating a Culture of Excellence,* app. A, College Station, 1999.

2. Reynolds interviews; "New Head Involved with Students: No Big Changes in Store for MSC," *Battalion,* May 7, 1980.

3. Reynolds interviews; Cid Galindo '85, interview by author, Austin, Tex., January 22, 2004; *Comprehensive Program Review of the Memorial Student Center* (2002), 7–8.

4. Jane Bailey, interview by author, College Station, Tex., April 20, 2005; Reynolds interviews; Wood quoted in "MSC Funds Raised by 12 Committees," *Battalion,* October 2, 1984; "How A&M's Student Union Works," *Bryan–College Station Eagle,* March 9, 1988; "Success Story: At Texas A&M's Memorial Student Center, 'Development' Means More Than Fund Raising," *ACU-I Bulletin,* July 1991, 5–8.

5. "Endowment to Support Ever-Growing Student Center Programs," *Texas Aggie,* December 1979; Noah quoted in "MSC Funds Raised by 12 Committees," *Battalion,* October 2, 1984.

6. James E. Wiley Sr. '46 and Virginia Wiley, interview by author, College Station,

Tex., September 5, 2003; "Wiley Lecture Series—History," http//wiley.tamu.edu/
history.html.

7. Black interview; Wiatt interview; David and Valerie Woodcock interview; "30 Years of OPAS," *Bryan–College Station Eagle,* September 1, 2002; *Comprehensive Program Review of the Memorial Student Center* (2002), 29.

8. Black interview.

9. *Aggieland,* 1980, 1981, 1985; "People, Places, and Programs," 2.

10. "The MSC—The On-Campus Land of Opportunity," *Bryan–College Station Eagle,* August 24, 1978; "Meeting the Challenge," MSC brochure, 1983; *Aggieland,* 1987, 59–65.

11. Bobby Bisor, interview by Dr. Haskell Monroe, College Station, Tex., October 4, 1999, 30–34, Cushing Memorial Library and Archives, Texas A&M University.

12. "The Memorial Student Center: A Look Inside," 57–59; "Cepheid Variable Builds on Unique Friendships," *Bryan–College Station Eagle,* May 20, 2006; "How NOVA Began," Association of Old Novads, http://ares.redsword.com/nova/origin.html; "Meeting the Challenge," MSC brochure, 1983.

13. Reynolds interview; Gibbs interview; Muller Jr. interview.

14. "Reagan Joins in Tribute to A&M's Stark," *Bryan–College Station Eagle,* November 10, 1985.

15. Stark tribute banquet program, November 9, 1985; Caperton interview; E. Lee Walker interview; Fitzhugh interview; James M. Howell, Cheryl Leavitt Haby, and James R. Reynolds to Friends of J. Wayne Stark, November 9, 1985, J. Wayne Stark Endowment for MSC Enrichment file, J. Wayne Stark biographical files, Memorial Student Center, Division of Student Affairs, Texas A&M University.

16. Marc Carroll '91, interview by author, Houston, Tex., November 19, 2003.

17. Reynolds interview; Bailey interview; Frank M. Muller III '88, interview by author, College Station, Tex., October 2, 2004; Muller Jr. interview; Fitzhugh interview, Jason Wilcox '91, interview by author, College Station, Tex., October 23, 2004.

18. Jessie (Mrs. Leland T.) Jordan, interview by Jane Bailey, Lufkin, Tex., n.d., MSC L. T. Jordan Institute, MSC files; "Jordan Collection Will Open at A&M" *Diboll (Tex.) Free Press,* November 27, 1986; "MSC Adds International Objects, Paintings to Special Collections," *Battalion,* July 1, 1987.

19. "Regents to Ponder Projects," *Bryan–College Station Eagle,* November 20, 1986; "A&M Committee Considers Plans for University Center Expansion," *Battalion,* October 7, 1987; "Regents Give Support of MSC Complex Plan," *Battalion,* July 14, 1988; "Board of Regents Considers Building Expansion, Parking," *Battalion,* August 29, 1988.

20. "The Memorial Student Center: A Look Inside," 11–12; "Boxed MSC Trees Suffer Shock," *Battalion,* July 26, 1990; "Professor's Prediction Comes True— Rudder Oak Transplant Fails," *Battalion,* August 22, 1990.

21. Douglas R. DeCluitt '57, telephone interview by author, March 29, 2005.

22. Reynolds interview; Reynolds, Presentation to the Executive Committee of the President's Commission on the Visual Arts, April 1, 1988; Jim Reynolds to Getty Foundation, addendum I, July 7, 1986.

23. "Aggie Donates Art Collection to A&M," *Battalion,* February 8, 1988; exhibit information for the Bill ('35) and Irma Runyon Art Collections, MSC Forsyth Center Galleries, MSC files.

24. Black interview; "Soviet Troupe Premieres Today," *Houston Chronicle,* November 23, 1990; "Aggieland beyond the Bolshoi," *Dallas Morning News,* November 18, 1990.

CHAPTER 5. THE CHALLENGES OF CHANGE

1. *Comprehensive Program of the Memorial Student Center* (2002), 7–10, 17–18; Texas A&M University, "Prospectus: Texas A&M University," Office of the Vice President for Research, October 2000; Reynolds interview.

2. Reynolds interview; F. James "Jimmy" Charney '96, interview by author, Austin, Tex., January 21, 2004; *Comprehensive Program Review of the Memorial Student Center* (2002), 8–9, 15.

3. "Faculty Recalls Stark's Deeds," *Battalion,* January 25, 1993.

4. Fitzhugh interview and his personal text of the eulogy.

5. Deryle Richmond, interview by author, College Station, Tex., April 20, 2005; James and Virginia Wiley interview; Memorial Student Center fundraising booklet, August 2006, MSC files.

6. "A&M Making Changes to Bring Reed Arena Out of the Red," *Bryan–College Station Eagle,* April 10, 2005; Reynolds interview; Bailey interview; "The MSC We Gave to A&M," *Texas Aggie,* February 1966, 14; Memorial Student Center fundraising booklet, August 2006.

7. Penny Ditton, interview by author, College Station, Tex., April 20, 2005; "Largest Student-Run Film Festival Gears Up for Seventh Year at Texas A&M," *Battalion,* February 15, 2000; "The Texas Film Festival Is the Largest Student Run Festival," *Animation World Network,* http://news.awn.com/index .php?&newsitem_no=4110; "Filmmaker Spike Lee Returns to Texas A&M University," *Aggie Daily,* April 11, 2001, Office of University Relations, Texas A&M University.

8. Texas A&M University, *Vision 2020.*

9. Luke J. Altendorf, interview by author, College Station, Tex., April 20, 2005.

10. Reynolds interview; Bailey interview; Altendorf interview, *Comprehensive Program Review of the Memorial Student Center* (2002), 18, 25.

11. "Leadership through the Ages: Senior Leaders of Tomorrow (MSC ALOT)," *MSC Extra,* spring 2005, MSC Council development newsletter, MSC files; Memorial Student Center fundraising booklet, August 2006.

12. Fitzhugh interview.

13. Bailey interview; "To Italy and Beyond," *MSC Extra,* fall 2004; Andy Liddell '06, quoted in Memorial Student Center fundraising booklet, August 2006.

14. Ditton interview; Memorial Student Center fundraising booklet, August 2006; "How It All Began," MSC FISH, http://fish.tamu.edu/History.

15. "Aggies Reaching Out: (MSC LEAD)," *MSC Extra,* spring 2005; Altendorf interview.

16. Charney interview.

17. Frank and Joanie Abbott, interview by author, College Station, Tex., September 26, 2003; Reynolds interview.

18. "Bruce Spencer '37," MSC Spencer Leadership Conference, http://spencer .tamu.edu/BruceSpencer.html.

19. Attendee quote from Memorial Student Center fundraising booklet, August 2006; Altendorf interview; Bailey interview.

20. Altendorf interview; Reynolds interview; Memorial Student Center fundraising booklet, August 2006; Texas A&M University, *Vision 2020.*

21. Reynolds interview; Altendorf interview; Nellson Burns '97, interview by author, Houston, Tex., April 21, 2006.

22. Altendorf interview; Reynolds interview; Bailey interview.

23. Reynolds interview; Black interview.

24. Altendorf interview; Memorial Student Center fundraising booklet, August 2006.

25. Ken Ballard '90, interview with author, Houston, Tex., January 23, 2007.

26. Reynolds interview; Altendorf interview.

27. Reynolds interview; Bailey interview; "Success Story" *ACU-I Bulletin,* 5–8.

28. Wilcox interview.

29. "Presentation to Student Service Fee Board, Spring 2005," April 28, 2005, Memorial Student Center Council, MSC files.

30. Bailey interview.

31. Ron Fulton '76, interview by author, College Station, Tex., August 6, 2004.

32. Reynolds interview; "More Than a Building—The MSC Celebrates 50 Years of Service," *Aggie Daily,* September 6, 2000, Office of University Relations, Texas A&M University.

33. *Comprehensive Program Review of the Memorial Student Center* (2002),10, 87; Reynolds interview; Altendorf interview.

34. R. N. "Dick" Conolly '37, interview by author, College Station, Tex., August 30, 2003; McNew interview.

35. Charney interview.

36. Arredondo interview.

37. Muller III interview.

38. Reynolds interview; "Four New 'Legends of Aggieland' Will Be Honored," *Aggie Daily,* September 28, 2000, Office of University Relations, Texas A&M University.

39. Luke Altendorf, telephone interview by author, February 18, 2008.

40. Flores interview.

41. Brent "B. R." Adams '89, telephone interview by author, March 21, 2005.

EPILOGUE

1. "Building on Tradition: MSC Renovation," *MSC Extra,* Fall 2007, 1, 5; "Revamping a Landmark," *Bryan–College Station Eagle,* October 7, 2007; "The Votes Are In: MSC Renovation Approved," *Battalion,* October 12, 2007; Altendorf interview, 2008.

2. "Texas A&M University Memorial Student Center Renovations," http://votemsc.tamu.edu/index.html; Altendorf interview, 2008.

Bibliography

Archival Sources

**Association of Former Students, Texas A&M University,
Clayton Williams Center, College Station, Tex.**

Alumni Quarterly, 1916–1921. *Directory of Former Students* collection. Minutes of
the Board of Directors of the Association of Former Students, 1880–2000. *Texas
Aggie* magazine collection, 1924–2000. *Texas A&M Review,* March 20, 1946.

**Biographical Files, Cushing Memorial Library and Archives,
Texas A&M University, College Station, Tex.**

J. Wayne Stark; Thomas O. Walton.

**Cushing Memorial Library and Archives,
Texas A&M University, College Station, Tex.**

Agenda Books of Board of Directors [Regents]. *Aggieland* yearbooks, 1941–2000.
"Buildings—Memorial Student Center," Special Subjects Folders. Dr. Haskell
Monroe interviews. East Bell County A&M Mothers' Club scrapbook. MSC
OPAS Scrapbooks. "MSC Programs–General," Special Subjects Folders.
President's Office Papers. Olin E. "Tiger" Teague Papers.

Memorial Student Center files, Division of Student Affairs, Texas A&M University, College Station, Texas.

Porter Butts files. *Comprehensive Program Review of the Memorial Student Center* (2002). Exhibit information for the Bill ('35) and Irma Runyon Art Collection, MSC Forsyth Center Galleries. Jessie (Mrs. Leland T.) Jordan interview by Jane Bailey. J. Wayne Stark Endowment history file. MSC Brochures file. *MSC Extra,* MSC Council development newsletter. MSC Council minutes. Memorial Student Center fundraising booklet, August 2006. President's Commission on the Visual Arts file. J. Wayne Stark files. YMCA Freshman Handbooks (1958–61).

Sterling C. Evans Library, Texas A&M University, College Station, Texas.

The Battalion, 1936–2008
The Bryan–College Station Eagle, 1954–2007

Books, Articles, and Manuscripts

Adams, Jr. John A. "Celebrating 125 Years, 1879–2004." *Directory of Former Students 2004,* 10–45. Association of Former Students, Texas A&M University.

————. *Keepers of the Spirit: The Corps of Cadets at Texas A&M University, 1876–2001.* College Station: Texas A&M University Press, 2001.

————. *We Are the Aggies: The Texas A&M University Association of Former Students.* College Station: Texas A&M University Press, 1979.

Aggie Daily. Office of University Relations, Texas A&M University.

"Aggieland beyond the Bolshoi." *Dallas Morning News,* November 18, 1990.

"Aggieland's Move to Opulence a Bad Gig." *San Antonio Light,* May 7, 1975.

"The Biggest Aggie Joke of All." *Texas Observer,* March 28, 1975.

Butts, Porter. *The College Union Idea: As Reflected, Principally in the Writings and Addresses of Porter Butts.* Bloomington, Ind.: Association of College Unions–International, 1971.

Dethloff, Henry C. *A Centennial History of Texas A&M University, 1876–1976.* College Station: Texas A&M University Press, 1975.

"Elegant Uproar at A&M." *Houston Post,* May 1, 1975.

"Ground Broken at Texas A&M for Memorial Student Center." *Fort Worth Star-Telegram,* September 22, 1948.

"Jordan Collection Will Open at A&M." *Diboll (Tex.) Free Press,* November 27, 1986.

Langford, Ernest. *Here We'll Build the College.* College Station: Texas A&M University, 1963.

"The Memorial Student Center: A Look Inside." Group project paper prepared by students of Gary Floden, PhD, Texas A&M University, Summer 1993.

Perry, George Sessions. *The Story of Texas A and M.* New York: McGraw-Hill, 1951.

"Scores of Visitors Are Present for Opening of Student Center." *Bryan News,* September 24, 1950.

"Six More Regional Conferences Set." *Association of College Unions Bulletin* 17 (December 1949): 1, 3.

"Success Story: At Texas A&M's Memorial Student Center, 'Development' Means More Than Fundraising." *Association of College Unions–International (ACU-I) Bulletin* (July 1991): 5–8.

Texas A&M University. "Prospectus: Texas A&M University." Office of the Vice President for Research. October 2000.

————. *Vision 2020: Creating a Culture of Excellence.* College Station, 1999.

Interviews by Author

Frank and Joanie Abbott, September 26, 2003
Dr. Carolyn Adair '69, October 25, 2007
Brent "B. R." Adams '89, March 21, 2005
Jodi Adcock '95, September 12, 2004
Luke J. Altendorf, April 20, 2005; February 18, 2008
Joe Arredondo '73, October 10, 2005
Jane Bailey, April 20, 2005
Ken Ballard '90, January 23, 2007
Anne T. Black, April 20, 2005
James "Jim" Briggs '80, September 11, 2003
Nellson Burns '97, April 21, 2006
Kent Caperton '71, January 22, 2004
Marc Carroll '91, November 19, 2003
Bill Carter '69, October 22, 2004
F. James "Jimmy" Charney '96, January 21, 2004
Don R. Cloud '59, October 8, 2003
R. N. "Dick" Conolly '37, August 30, 2003
Bill Davis '75, November 13, 2004
Douglas R. DeCluitt '57, March 29, 2005
Penny Ditton, April 20, 2005
Fred Dollar '44, November 12, 2004
Paul Dresser '64, September 6, 2006
Chet Edwards '74, September 27, 2006
Curtis Feeny '79, September 17, 2003
Thomas C. Fitzhugh III '71, October 22, 2003
William H. "Bill" Flores '76, November 10, 2003
Ron Fulton '76, August 6, 2004
Cid Galindo '85, January 22, 2004
Jarrell H. Gibbs '60, August 30, 2003
Lynn Gibson '77, July 31, 2004
Sam Gillespie '81, October 23, 2004
Rachel Gonzales, September 11, 2004
Colonel Robert F. Gonzales '68, September 11, 2004
Hector Gutierrez Jr. '69, January 23, 2004
Jon L. Hagler '58, September 11, 2004
Robert Hall '63, September 27, 2003
Robert W. Harvey '77, October 30, 2007
Dr. Howard Head '64, March 28, 2005
Heather Hartman '93, September 12, 2004
Bill Hensel '41, September 18, 2004
James B. "Dick" Hervey '42, October 27, 2003
William B. "Bill" Heye Jr. '60, October 1, 2004
Joe Horn '63, November 7, 2003
James M. Howell '56, April 23, 2004
John W. Jenkins '56, October 25, 2003
Dr. Fran Kimbrough '69, November 14, 2004
Dr. John J. Koldus III, August 5, 2004
Weldon D. Kruger '53, September 16, 2005
Bill Lancaster '49, December 19, 2003
Sanders Letbetter, September 18, 2004

John H. Lindsey '44, September 24, 2003
Drew McGehee '93, August 7, 2004
Sallie McGehee, August 7, 2004
Dr. J. T. L. "Lamar" McNew '53, October 25, 2003
Dr. Haskell Monroe, August 5, 2004
Frank M. Muller Jr. '65, September 4, 2003
Frank M. Muller III '88, October 2, 2004
Charles Parker '55, March 16, 2005
Wayne Prescott '69, January 22, 2004
Jack M. Rains '60, February 7, 2005
Patrick G. "Pat" Rehmet '68, August 24, 2004
James R. "Jim" Reynolds, October 28, 2005, and April 18, 2006
Deryle Richmond, April 20, 2005
Ray Rothrock '77, December 10, 2003
John S. Samuels III '54, October 18, 2003
John Sharp '72, September 8, 2004
Colonel Vance Shaw, October 19, 2006
Pat Spillman '49, August 21, 2003
Richard R. "Dick" Tumlinson '51, October 6, 2003
E. Lee Walker '64, March 17, 2004
Robert L. "Bob" Walker '58, February 18, 2004
Don A. Webb '71, November 12, 2004
John Whitmore III '51, June 7, 2004
Herbert W. "Bud" Whitney '56, October 25, 2003
Ann Wiatt, September 9, 2006
Jason Wilcox '91, October 23, 2004
James E. Wiley Sr. '46 and Virginia Wiley, September 5, 2003
David Woodcock and Valerie Woodcock, September 2, 2006
Anne Elizabeth Wynn '86, January 24, 2004
Will Wynn '84, January 24, 2004

Index

While an undergraduate at Texas A&M
University, AMY L. BACON '91 served
as the vice president of development for
the Memorial Student Center. She holds
a Master's degree in public history from
the University of Houston.

NUMBER 110
*Centennial Series of the Association of
Former Students,*
Texas A&M University

COVER PHOTO: MSC Flag Room,
courtesy MSC Development.

"This is the story of the "other education" that Texas Aggies receive at Texas A&M University. The Memorial Student Center (MSC) is a living memorial that serves both to preserve and honor the past while facilitating change, enrichment, and the diversification of the unique culture of Aggieland. It is a community center, a leadership laboratory, and a spiritual center—and with the Corps of Cadets, is at the core of the total Aggie life experience. And this is a story that has never been told."

—**HENRY DETHLOFF**, author, *Texas Aggies Go to War*

"Sometimes a building takes on a life of its own. You know what I mean. When someone mentions it by name you easily relate. The sight of it evokes a sense of calm acquaintance and when you take off your hat and walk inside, its unique aroma stirs memory, emotion, and hope. That is what Amy Bacon's terrific rendition, *Building Leaders, Living Tradition* did for me. The MSC is as much a tradition on the Texas A&M campus as the Aggie Ring or Muster. It is the physical heart of Aggieland that invokes and inspires so much of our spirit. Amy tells it the right way, through the people who both guided and absorbed the 'C.'"

—**EDDIE J. DAVIS** '67, president, Texas A&M Foundation

"At the heart of Texas A&M University, the Memorial Student Center is a special place where education and character-building continue to occur for so many Aggies."

—**JOHN H. LINDSEY**, Class of '44

ISBN-13: 978-1-60344-095-0
ISBN-10: 1-60344-095-X

52000

9 781603 440950